Creative Guitar 3

Recording Effects

Printed and bound in the UK by MPG Books Ltd, Bodmin, Cornwall

Published in the UK by SMT, an imprint of Sanctuary Publishing Limited, Sanctuary House, 45–53 Sinclair Road, London W14 0NS, United Kingdom

www.sanctuarypublishing.com

Copyright: Phil Hilborne and Ace, 2003

Cover image courtesy of Richard Ecclestone
Music typesetting: Cambridge Notation

ISBN: 1-84492-011-9

Creative Guitar 3

Recording Effects

Phil Hilborne and Ace

smt

BOOK CONTENTS

CD CONTENTS

1 **Intro From Phil And Ace**

Chapter 1
2 **Reverb Examples**
   a) Small Reverb
   b) Plate Reverb
   c) Dual Amplifier Spring Type Reverb
   d) Small Room Reverb
   e) Small Hall Reverb
   f) Cathedral-Size Reverb
   g) Immense-Size Reverb (played with volume control swells)
   h) Large-Arena-Size Reverb (fingerstyle electric *à la* Jeff Beck)
   i) Plate Reverb

3 **Reverb Demo Piece Intro**

4 **Reverb Demo Piece**
   Incorporating Volume Control Swells, Large Reverb And Reverse Reverb Lead-Guitar Lines

Chapter 2
5 **Distortion Intro**

6 **Distortion Examples**
   a) Preamp Distortion
   b) Overdrive
   c) Fuzz
   d) Distortion

Chapter 3
7 **Wah Intro**

8 **Wah Examples**
   a) Rhythmic Clean Wah
   b) Rhythmic Muted Wah
   c) *Shaft*-Style Wah
   d) Conversational-Style Wah
   e) Wah As Tone (Fixed Position)

   f) Wah Lead
   g) Accented Wah Lead
   h) Distortion After Wah
   i) Distortion Before Wah

9 **Wah Demo Piece Intro**

10 **Wah Demo**

Chapter 4
11 **Modulation 1 Intro**

12 **Chorus Examples**
   a) Mono Chorus
   b) Stereo Chorus
   c) Chorus Echo
   d) Distortion/Chorus

13 **Flanger Examples**
   a) Tape Flange
   b) Flange And Distortion
   c) Slow Flange
   d) Slow Flange (Muted Guitar)

14 **Phaser Examples**
   a) Deep Phaser (Dirty Sound)
   b) Classic Phaser (Clean Sound)

Chapter 5
15 **Pitch Effects Intro**

16 **Pitch Effects Intro**
   a) Detuned Pitch Shift (*à la* Eddie Van Halen)
   b) Twin Lead Style Pitch Shift
   c) Unison plus Octave Lead
   d) Triad Lead Phrase (*à la* Brian May)
   e) 12 String Effect 1 (down an octave and up a fifth)
   f) 12 String Effect 2 (up an octave and detuned)
   g) 12 String Effect 3 (up an octave twice)
   h) Classic (BOSS) Octaver

CD produced, compiled/edited by Phil Hilborne. Mastered by Phil Hilborne.

Recorded/mixed by Phil Hilborne at WM Studios, Essex, October 2003.

Phil Hilborne – All guitars and composition except for the VG88 demos (Jerry Stephenson), the voicebox demo (Geoff Whitehorn) and the XP300 demos (Ace).

Phil Hilborne – all programming/editing. Phil Hilborne uses and endorses PRS and Fret King Guitars, Picato Strings and Marshall and Cornford amplification.

Ace uses and endorses products by PRS guitars, AMT and Cornford Amps.

Drum samples were taken from 'Burning Grooves' – used under licence from Spectronics. Drum loops by Abe Laboriel Jr, courtesy of Spectronics' 'Burning Grooves'.

www.philhilborne.com/www.acesounds.com

ACKNOWLEDGEMENTS

We would like to thank the following people and companies for helping to make this book possible.

All at *Guitarist* magazine

All at *Guitar Techniques* magazine

All at Line 6

All at DigiTech and Arbiter, Neil, Nick, Danny, Jo

Richard Ecclestone

Bruce Dickinson, Damian and all at BIMM

All at BOSS

Terry and Simon at PMT

Paul Airey at Hughes & Kettner

All at Pedaltrain

Pete Lunney at Strings and Things

Snails Pace Slim and The Hamsters

Gary at Sounds Great

Rob Harris from Jamiroquai

Geoff Whitehorn from Procol Harum

PRS Guitars: Gavin Mortimer

Fret King Guitars: Trevor Wilkinson

Neville Marten

Jerry Stephenson

Mike Hill

Adrian Legg

Chris at Rhodes Music

Asia Musik Technology: Andrew Marikev, Don Cowie

Gibson Keddie

Snarling Dogs

Jamie Crompton from Fender Foreword

All at Celestion UK Ltd

EMS Ltd

All at Guitar Mania

Lewis Brangwyn and Alan Heal

Jim Marshall and Steve Yelding at Marshall Amplification

Nicko McBrain from Iron Maiden

MOTU UK

Paul Remmington

Alan Hutton

Tony Gravel

All at TASCAM UK

Tony Muschamp and JJ Guitars

Dave Gladden

Jan Cyrka

Chris Francis and Cambridge Notation

Brian May, Laurie Wisefield, Alan Darby, Neil Murray, Andy Jones, Mike Dixon, Elliot Ware, Emma Sainsbury, Andy Smith, Tony Bourke, Ben Milton and All at *We Will Rock You*

All at Cornford Amplification

Phil Castang

All at the IGF

All at Sound Technology plc

Stu, Kim and all at Jamtrax/Total Accuracy

Clive Moreton, Tim Slater and all at MB Publishing

INTRODUCTION

Welcome to our crazy world of effects pedals and units. This book is essentially a layman's guide to using and experimenting with all the major guitar effects groups. It's not a technical manual telling you the specifications of transistors and wave oscillators, but a simple guide to achieving the best results with the most ease and fun with what you have. Throughout its pages, we'll tell you how things are done and also illustrate a few tricks, but the main thing to remember when experimenting with sound is that it's all in the way you hear it. As legendary '60s producer Joe Meek once said, 'If it sounds right, it is right!'

Over the years, we've had lots of fun with effects, from re-inventing the standard guitar sound to creating alien soundscapes, which has always amused us and kept our interest in playing fresh. We've included simple recording techniques here to start you off, plus a few off-the-wall applications of effects from the road less travelled by most guitarists. The accompanying CD is a great reference for understanding sounds, right up to learning new musical ideas from the scores and chord shapes included in this book and then applying them to your own style of playing.

Bear in mind that even before you consider adding effects there are various techniques that you can employ just by using your guitar and amp to achieve basic core sounds that can then be manipulated with effects. It's always best to start off with a good basic guitar sound and tone, which should then be combined with various pickup selections, volume-control changes and different playing techniques. Also, having good-quality guitar leads, such as Monster Cable, will help to produce a clearer, better-quality tone from your amp, as the signal from the guitar will be stronger and cleaner.

There are a few crazy words and metaphors describing the sounds of some effects, but that's the best way we can explain it simply and understandably. When they wrote the dictionary, effects pedals hadn't been invented! So our advice is to go create, have fun, and remember that it all ends up as far as you take it...

Ace
Phil Hilborne
2003

1 REVERB: DIGITAL AND SPRING

Arguably the most widely used effect is reverb, a very taken-for-granted, under-rated and often overlooked signal processor that can be found built into everything from amplifiers and recording desks to computer-recording plug-ins pretty much as standard. It is one of the most simplistic and organic-sounding effects, and probably – particularly given the minimal effort required to achieve great-sounding results – the all-time mood creator. Reverb creates the overall three-dimensional image within a recording; essentially it is a way of making the instrument sound as if it's being played in a different-sized room, according to the setting you choose, which can vary from a chicken shack to a cathedral.

The way in which sound is reflected off the surfaces – walls, ceiling and so on – of a room is called *reverberation*. Real-life reverb is basically a combination of millions of tiny echoes that fade away over a period of time according to the size and reflective nature of the space.

On an amplifier, the settings controlling the reverb can be as simple as a single knob with which you adjust the overall depth of the effect (the size of the hall, if you like). You may also be able to adjust the volume of the effect (in other words, how much of the effect is added to your original sound, with the size of the virtual hall increasing as you turn it up). Examples of amps with these features include the Fender Twin and the Cornford Hurricane combo. Blues and mood players can easily create a vintage club or hall-gig vibe, either in the studio or live.

The more depth you add to a reverb, the larger the hall becomes and the more distant and 'wet' the guitar sounds. On more complex reverbs, the terminology changes to hall sizes, or *plates*. The terms given to hall sizes are easy to understand: small room, concert hall, arena, and so on. The term *plates* means essentially the same thing, but you're more likely to hear it bandied about in a professional recording studio. You'll eventually learn to distinguish between the different types of reverb simply by listening to them and experimenting.

This reflection of sound can be altered by different *parameters* (changeable settings within the overall sound of the effect). For example, to create one reverb setting you may have three parameters to play with: volume, depth, and decay time. You'll encounter parameters on pretty much all effect racks and pedals, so it's essential to understand what this word refers to when reading operating manuals.

With reverb units, you can add as much of the effect as you like in order to create the desired mood, from subtle room emulation and massive expanses to ghostly chords and distant, heartbreaking solos. The controls are usually sufficiently sensitive to enable you to create very subtle effects with very small adjustments. The most basic parameters of reverb are listed below:

- **Volume** – This is the degree (or volume) of effect that is applied to the sound. In recording situations, it is often referred to as *wet* (referring to the effected signal added to the original sound) and *dry* (no effect, with the guitar sounding very close). Basically, volume determines how much of the added effect you hear.

- **Depth** – This parameter determines the size of the room you want to emulate. The more you increase the depth, the bigger the listener perceives the room to be.

- **Decay Time** – Once a sound is generated in a room, the various reflected sound waves take differing lengths of time to become inaudible, or *decay*. This is emulated via the decay time parameter, which determines for how long these waves will continue to be heard.

You may find more – or, indeed, fewer – functions on various types of reverb units, but these are the fundamental parameters you'll encounter even when using the effect on a very simplistic level. It's really not rocket science, this one, and maybe that's why reverb is so universally used, but the right application of this effect – from subtle to insane – can create the make-or-break sound, setting or mood for a player or a composition.

Where It's Used And Why

If you listen to a lot of records, you'll notice that reverb is applied to all of the instruments in a band, including the vocals. In the studio, guitar tracks are generally recorded in a very sterile (dry) environment, and adding reverb can add lush depth to any guitar track, bringing it to life.

Reverb is also used to create space and 'take a mix back' from sounding too close and aggressive. It creates space for other instruments to find their own natural places in the audio spectrum and lends a live feel to the music, emulating a gig or small rehearsal room and vice versa. Not adding reverb to a mix makes the music seem incredibly close-up and immediate to the listener, creating aggressive and very attention-grabbing personal moods. When you're talking about mixes, remember that an entire mix in itself can also be termed as 'dry' or 'wet'.

Most mixes combine dry and wet sounds on individual instruments to balance the music and find all the right spaces for melodies and hooks to breathe within the composition. A classic example of this is Peter Green's guitar solo on Fleetwood Mac's 'Albatross'. Swamped in reverb, it gives a distant and floating atmosphere to the track. Current trends are to apply less reverb than was common over the last 40 years of its life, but nevertheless it's still one of the most essential of all effects.

Types Of Reverb Unit

Reverb units can vary from the BOSS RV2 digital reverb pedal to the Lexicon 482 studio rack unit for mixing – which, incidentally, costs thousands of pounds.

The first – and among the most authentic-sounding – reverbs ever made were spring reverbs, which are still as popular as ever. Although not as reliable as its digital counterpart, the spring reverb consists of a spring in a tube which vibrates and resonates when activated, creating the rich, warm, thick tone preferred by purists. They are large and expensive units and usually come installed in the more expensive new amplifiers, or old amps manufactured before the advent of digital technology. They are also available as separate units. Unfortunately, in the authors' experience they do not travel well and constantly yield to the trials of life on the road. But when an authentic '50s or '60s sound is desired, spring reverbs are the real deal.

When an amp is in use and is accidentally knocked or kicked, this type of reverb creates a banging noise similar to a small explosion in a hall, which some guitarists actually use to create moods within songs by kicking the amplifier. This technique – for want of a better word – has been recognised by several manufacturers of digital pedals and can be found as a built-in feature on the Danelectro DSR-1 Spring King, for example, which has a pad that can be kicked to emulate this noise. How about that? They think of everything...

Settings

The various reverb parameters we looked at earlier are the ones you'll need to know to get started with most basic reverb units. More sophisticated units, such as rack-mount studio processors, will have additional parameters:

- **Type** – This refers to the type of room that you want to emulate.

- **Diffusion** – This simulates the effect of reflections coming from different materials in a typical room. Low diffusion settings are good for rooms with hard, flat surfaces, and high diffusion settings are good for simulating the presence of irregular materials such as natural rock masonry or man-made diffusers.

- **Tone** – This offers basic EQ adjustment.

The BOSS RV-3 Digital Reverb Delay pedal

Tips

In the studio, you can add reverb to create space and complement the recording or to create certain ambiences and moods that suit your particular project. For live use, though, don't get caught using too much, as even small rooms have their own natural reverb. Overuse will make the guitar all but disappear.

A few classic reverb units past and present include the BOSS RV-2 Digital Reverb, the BOSS RV-3 Digital Reverb Delay, and the Electro-Harmonix Holy Grail and Holier Grail. DigiTech produced the XP 400 Reverberator, and Danelectro served up the splendid Corned Beef. Also available out there are the Fender Twin Spring reverb, DigiTech's DigiVerb and the EBS Dynaverb.

2 DISTORTION, OVERDRIVE, FUZZ AND PREAMPS

Probably the most commonly owned group of pedals of all time are distortions, overdrives and fuzz boxes. They are essential in the evolution of rock and are responsible for some of the most aggressive and extreme guitar sounds ever! Most guitarists own a similar unit of some description, or if not they'll have an amplifier with a gain section or multiple gain channels.

Getting a good, distorted guitar sound is an essential part of creating your own unique style. Most famous guitarists have their own trademark sounds that stem from their distorted sound. From Smashing Pumpkins to Jimi Hendrix, distortion, fuzz and overdrive have shaped the expressive tonal qualities of generations of rock guitarists. Players far and wide strive and struggle to obtain the ultimate distorted sound. The ambiences of overdriven sounds are as varied as hairstyles, each designed to suit the character and individuality of the player. There is no right or wrong, just what turns you on and works for your situation and setup. The four variations covered here are distortion units, fuzz boxes, overdrive pedals and amplifier preamp gain sections.

Distortion units basically have all the characteristics of the other three. A distortion pedal or unit is a standalone box that emulates the preamp gain section of a tube amp that's 'wound up' (ie pushed until the valves are 'clipping', thus distorting of the signal). The effect was discovered way back in the 1950s, when guitarists used to turn up their amps louder than recommended by the manufacturer, thus creating the birth of blues solos and rock 'n' roll as we know it today.

Uses
Distortion
Distortion pedals are mainly used for changing from clean live sounds to a heavier, more aggressive sound and feel, or for allowing guitar solos to sustain and cut through more. Indeed, on some old pedals the distortion setting is referred to as 'sustain'. They can be added to already distorted ('gained', 'dirty' or 'overdriven') amps to increase the drive of the amp and produce excessive amounts of sustain and aggression. They can also be used to create feedback, which is, in fact, a guitar effect in itself.

Fuzz boxes are very similar to distortion in their function, and indeed people often use the same word for both. You might hear the sound that they produce referred to as *brown sound*. In our opinion, fuzz boxes are a bit cruder than distortion units and have a type of 'clipping' effect more along the lines of '60s and '70s guitar tones. Many of the designs are more groovy and crazy, implying more way-out tones than those of its more serious cousin, distortion.

Fuzz pedals tend to be more varied in their tones from manufacturer to manufacturer. The sound is a bit more extreme, unique and...well...a bit more *fuzzy*. Many great '60s guitar heroes owe their top moments to bizarre fuzz pedals such as the Colorsound Tone Bender and the Electro-Harmonix Big Muff.

Fuzz
Fuzz boxes have fundamentally the same applications as distortion units, although in more recent years many guitarists have added them to the overdriven amp setting to create massive-sounding riffs and searing solos. Their characteristics make them a bit wilder and dirtier, producing a more unreasonable tone with which to scare the neighbours.

Overdrive
Overdrive pedals have two main uses: to overdrive ('push') a clean amp in order to produce crunchy rhythms of slightly distorted guitar sounds, or to push the already gained preamp section of an amp to increase the distortion and produce a fat-rock/heavy-metal riffing sound.

An overdrive unit will produce a smoother distortion on an already gained amp than either a fuzz or distortion pedal as the internal drive circuitry of the pedal is not as extreme ('hot'). An overdrive – when used correctly – can drive the amp harder to produce more sustain and distortion without changing the tonal characteristics of the amp's original sound. Another application is to use it to make the guitar more responsive and 'easier to play' without noticeably changing the sound.

One of the most famous overdrive pedals is the Ibanez TS9 Tube Screamer used by guitarists of all musical styles from Stevie Ray Vaughan to Skunk Anansie.

The number of features found on overdrive pedals will vary between models and manufacturers, from simple two-knob operation to full-on EQ and programmable memory banks. The most common features are outlined below.

- **Level** – Controls the overall output volume when the effect is applied.
- **Drive, Distortion, Fuzz, Sustain, Gain, Boost** – Controls the amount of effect applied to the dry signal.
- **Tone, Colour Mix, Contour, Punch, Fat, Muscle, High, Low, Bass, Middle, Treble** – These are all EQ controls which you can set to suit your ear and taste. These controls will vary on different models of overdrive.

A significant drawback to overdrive pedals is that they can generate a lot of extra line noise and feedback – they are by far the noisiest pedals of the bunch! However, there are a few ways of controlling this, such as switching a unit on only when it is needed or using a noise gate to shut off the signal to the amp when the effect is switched on but you're not playing through it. We'll cover various noise gates in a later section of this book.

There are literally hundreds of overdrive boxes available today, as well plenty of vintage models, but the following list and illustrations spotlight some of the better ones on the market.

Common Effects Units
Overdrive

- BOSS OD-1 Overdrive, OD-2 Turbo Overdrive, SD-1 Super Overdrive, OD-20
- Colorsound Powerboost
- Marshall Guvnor
- DOD FX102 Mystic Overdrive, FX101 Grind, FX100 Integrated Tube, 250 Overdrive Preamp
- Danelectro Daddy O, Pastrami
- Electro-Harmonix Hot Tubes
- Ibanez Tube Screamer
- BOSS BD-2 Blues Drive
- Hughes & Kettner Tube Factor
- DigiTech XTD Tone Driver
- Jacques Tube Blower
- Tube Works Shred, Rock Tube
- Frontline Overdrive. Danelectro

Distortion

- DOD FX55 Supra distortion, FX69 Grunge, FX86 Death Metal Distortion
- Pro Co Rat & Vintage Rat
- Ibanez SM9 Super Metal, PDS1
- BOSS HM-2 Heavy Metal, DS-1 Distortion, HM-3 Hyper Metal, XT-2 Xtortion, DS-2 Turbo Distortion, MT-2 Metal Zone, MZ-2 Digital Metalizer
- Snarling Dogs-Blue Doo, Fuzz Buzz, Black Dog
- AMT DistStation
- Danelectro Black Coffee, Grilled Cheese, T-Bone, Bacon 'n' Eggs, Black Licorice
- Frantone The Sweet
- NGCS Dirt Box
- AMT Fatal Tube

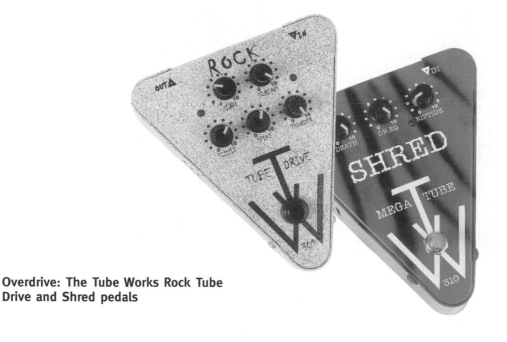

Overdrive: The Tube Works Rock Tube Drive and Shred pedals

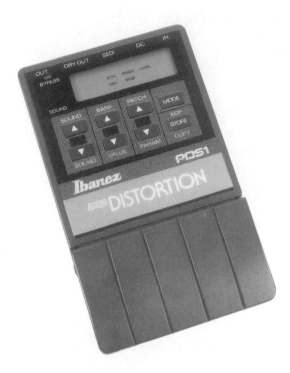

Distortion: the Ibanez PDS1

Overdrive: Marshall's The Guv'nor

Fuzz

- Colorsound Tone Bender
- Electro-Harmonix Big Muff, Graphic Fuzz
- Snarling Dogs Tweed E Dog
- Danelectro Fab Tone
- Frantone Peach Fuzz and Cream Puff

- Dallas Arbiter Fuzz Face
- BOSS FZ-3 Fuzz, Hyper Fuzz
- Vox Tone Bender
- Z-Vex Fuzz Factory
- DOD FX76 Punkifier
- Jacques Fuse Blower

Overdrive: DOD Integrated Tube

Distortion: the Ibanez Super Metal

More Uses
Preamps

A close relative to the overdrive family is the preamp pedal, which also comes as a rack unit. Preamps are used for shaping the tone at the front end of the amp from the guitar. All amps have preamp sections on them, unless they are power amps or 'slave' units. Preamps generally have EQ sections of treble, middle and bass, plus gain and volume controls. (Gain is the amount of drive/distortion added to the signal at the front end.) In pedal or rack form, they are used either to shape the guitar tone/sound for use with a power amp (which has no EQ or drive section) or to add tone to an already 'flat' (ie neutral EQ'd) amp. They are also commonly used to push and 'wind up' already-gained amps to produce fat, natural, super gain distortion with rich harmonics.

Some preamps boast valve circuitry, which will give a hotter, richer dynamic in sound, while others are solid-state driven for reliability and cost and some are a mixture of both. Most multi-FX units contain them, too.

A while back, preamps were simple affairs with usually one channel of EQ and in and out sockets. These days they are complex switching units with up to four channels of programmable separate EQ and drives. We'll try to explain here what they basically do by providing examples of how we would use them. In short, they can be used to achieve a better clean sound in terms of rhythm crunch, rhythm heavy gain and solo lead gain.

Distortion: the BOSS Heavy Metal HM-2

Distortion: the NGCS Dirtbox

- Preamps can be used to enhance a clean sound on a flat or lifeless-sounding amp by using the EQ section and a tiny amount of gain to bring life, definition and sparkle to the sound.

- A power amp's preamp section can shape the guitar sound/tone by setting EQ for clean and distorted channels separately. Adding drive to the distorted channels creates a sound suitable for rhythm playing and solos.

- On a clean amp that has no gain or drive control, a preamp can be used to achieve natural-sounding distortion and boost for solos.

- On an amp that has limited gain, such as a Marshall JCM 800, a preamp can push the original valve sound in the gain section to overload, creating more natural distortion and harmonics without changing the characteristics of the amp tone.

- A preamp can obtain massive gains and boosts on solos that need loads of distortion and sustain.

- With a programmable or multi-channel preamp unit you can switch between degrees of drive and clean sounds effortlessly if you have a single-channel amplifier.

For over ten years, New York-based company Tech 21 has been producing pedal and rack preamps of superior quality which have now become a standard feature in studios all over the world. They range from emulating classic amplifier preamp drive sections to state-of-the-art programmable modelling racks. Models currently available include the SansAmp Classic, SansAmp GT2, TRI-OD, SansAmp Bass Driver DI, SansAmp Acoustic DI, SansAmp PSA-1, and SansAmp TRI-AC.

Mesa Boogie manufactures some world-class multi-channel rack units, including the Triaxis and the V2 pedal. Marshall introduced the classic JMP1 rack many years ago and Rocktron followed with their Prophesy model, plus more recently the Gainiac and Voodoo Valve. Other pedal preamps currently available include the Koch Pedal Tone, Bad Cat 2 Tone, AMT DistStation, DOD 250 Preamp Overdrive, Art Acoustic Preamp, BOSS FA-1 FET Amplifier and the Hughes & Kettner TubeMan.

Fuzz: Colour Sound Tone Bender

Fuzz: Electro-Harmonix Big Muff

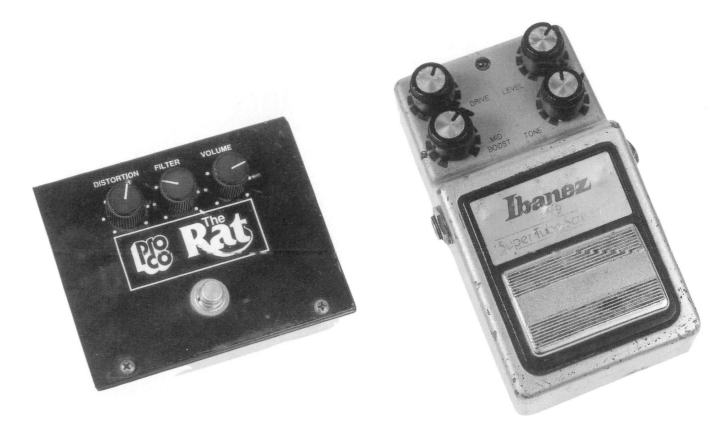

Fuzz: Pro Co's The Rat

Overdrive: the Ibanez Tube Screamer

Fuzz: Danelectro Fab Tone

3 WAH-WAH, AUTOWAH AND ENVELOPE FILTERS

A classic and instantly recognisable member of the effects family is the wah-wah pedal. An integral part of funky rhythms and screaming metal solos, it can breathe life and fire into any guitar player's style. The wah has had many offshoots over the years and is often used in crazy combinations with other effects.

The wah is basically a variable-frequency filter foot expression pedal, controlled manually by the sweeping action of the player's foot in an up-and-down fashion. This means that, as you move the pedal up and down, you change the tone of the note, creating an expressive wah-wah sound. How you choose to use it is entirely up to you – wah can make you sound like the King of Funk or the Lord of the Screaming Solo!

For ultra-funky rhythms from the '70s (or, as it is known to some, a *Shaft* style, named after an Isaac Hayes tune from a famous '70s detective film), we would recommend setting the amp on a relatively clean sound. First, turn the wah on by pushing forward to activate it, and then bring the pedal back with your heel. Play a medium-to-fast, percussive, semi-muted chopping rhythm and then slowly – maybe in half time – sweep the pedal from heel to toe. Try to land in the toe position when you hit a downstroke. This is a very funky effect and can be played using either a clean or dirty-sounding amp, depending on how aggressive you want to get. Check out the CD demos (Track 8) to hear this technique in use.

When it comes to using wah during solos, it's a simple matter of feeling the notes and opening and closing the pedal when you want to make the note either sing out or moan. As you push your toe forward to the open filter position, the note will become sharper and more piercing, thus becoming more expressive and 'singing'. In the heel position, the notes will 'honk'. Jimmy Page used this idea on the intro to Led Zeppelin's 'No Quarter'. Jimi Hendrix's 'Voodoo Chile' illustrates masterful use of wah on its intro, and you should also check out solos and melodies by Joe Satriani and Steve Vai.

Some blues and rock players use the wah in set positions back from the toe for whole sections or solos. This backs off the treble and creates a mood for the piece; by opening and closing the filter slightly you can create subtle textures to suit the feel of the particular moment, a technique for which Michael Schenker, of UFO and The Scorpions, was well known. Another technique is to play a note or chord and to sweep up and down very quickly, creating a tremolo 'swamp' feel.

Finally, where you decide to place the wah in your signal chain has a radical effect on the wah's sound. If the wah is placed before a preamp gain or a fuzz/distortion unit, you will obtain the regular sweet tone of the filter thinning the notes, but if the wah is placed after distortion it will produce a thick whoosh like a huge gust of wind. Seventies acid-rock band Hawkwind used this sound a lot, and while it's not preferred by many, it's great when used in the right place. Give it a try! These techniques are also on the CD.

The wah is a pedal that you definitely have to 'feel' when using, as you're actively controlling the expression of your notes with it.

Most analogue wahs have a switch at the front that activates the effect, and a pot (short for potentiometer) that is turned by the foot action and changes the filter frequency. These pots and switches can become crackly or noisy after years of operation and should be cleaned regularly with switch cleaner. Morley Effects manufactures a range of light-cell-activated wahs, thus eliminating the crackly pots and switches, although some players prefer these. Mark Tremonti from Creed has a signature model, as does Steve Vai.

Jim Dunlop (Crybaby), Morley and Vox produce some of the classic wah sounds recognised today. Others include the Snarling Dogs Wino, Moldspore, Bluesbawl and Blackbawl models; Danelectro's Dan O Wah; DOD's FX17 Wah Volume; Colorsound Wah; BOSS's FW-3 Footwah and PW-10; Roger Mayer's Vision Wah; Tech 21's Killer Wail; Real McCoy's RMC3; and the Vox V847.

Auto-wah is basically a wah filter controlled automatically by the pedal when it's activated, thus removing all the legwork. The auto-wah uses a sensitivity detector that reads the input signal of the guitar and then simulates the action of a manual wah pedal. When you pick with an aggressive attack, the note is radically altered, but a more delicate tone is obtained when you play with a softer touch. Most auto-wahs have knobs for 'sensitivity' (when you want the filter to start to open in relation to the attack of your picking) and 'peak' (how far you want the filter to open once it's activated). Other models may include knobs labelled 'range' instead of sensitivity, and on some the peak control is called 'sensitivity', although it'll only take you a few seconds to realise this once you've played a note. Two classic auto-wahs are the T-Wah (TW1, formerly

known as the Touch Wah) and the Auto Wah (AW2), both from BOSS). Also available are the Z-Vex Seek Wah and Danelectro French Fries.

Another wing in the army of wah pedals comprises the hybrid combinations that mix wah filtering with other known effects pedals to create exciting and crazy results. Wah-wah fuzz has been very popular for years across all the brands, and also wah volume (swell) too. Here are a few to wet the taste buds from recent times, but the list can be endless, especially as vintage weirdos pop up all the time.

Charlie Stringer's Snarling Dogs made a range of wahs pedal that were fashioned in the shape of a bare foot and where the wah effect was combined with a fuzz, a ring

Jim Dunlop Crybaby Wah

modulator or a distortion, with three settings of filters on each model: Shaft ('70s style), Voodoo (Jimi Hendrix style) and White Room (Eric Clapton in Cream style). Models include the Mold Spore (with ring modulator), WinoWah (with boost) and BluesBall (with tube emulating distortion).

Danelectro has produced retro-style wahs including fuzz and octave dividers combined – for a '60s vibe – with '50s car design styles. Models include the DW1 Dan O Wah (fuzz and octave) and TripL Wah (combinations of retro and modern filters).

Envelope Filters

Envelope filters are really in a bracket of their own in terms of how they work and what they do, but they are also very similar in sound to wah and auto-wah effects. Envelope filters open and close an 'envelopes' of frequencies automatically, governed by the settings you give it. They are triggered by how hard you hit the note when you pick (which opens the frequency sweep) and close at a rate determined by the user. The effect sounds almost if you're pressing a wah down as you play the note but then bringing it straight back to the heel position instantly, producing a funky squawk or vicious rock stab. Envelope Filters are probably more well known by bassists for the funky '70s tones that Bootsy Collins used to produce.

One of the first envelope filters was the Bassballs, by Electro-Harmonix, which had just one knob for sensitivity adjustment. At around the same time, the same company manufactured the Doctor Q for the guitar. Many '70s funk grooves used this effect, and now Electro-Harmonix has produced the Q-Tron, Mini Q-Tron and Q-Tron+ – modern versions of the original classic.

The envelope filtering effect can be great for quick bursts of wah when you don't want to flip the wah pedal on and

Vox Wah

off or you don't have time to do so. It's also a great way to manipulate funky riffs, using dynamics to make the guitar breathe and wail in an almost speech-like manner. Two tracks that feature good distorted wah examples are 'Justin' by Korn (from their *Follow The Leader* album) and Skunk Anansie's 'It Takes Blood And Guts' (on the *Paranoid And Sunburnt* LP), while a great funky clean example using the Mu-Tron 3 can be heard on the '70s Stevie Wonder hit 'Higher Ground'.

There are many envelope filters available on the market today, and while they all use slightly different terminology to describe their individual sounds, they all generally do the same thing, although some sound a lot fatter than others.

Probably the strangest effect in this genre was developed in the '70s and named the Soul Kiss, a unique envelope filter that features a sensor on the end of a hardwired cord instead of a pedal. You can put this sensor in your mouth, under your arm or in your hand, and by opening and closing that part of the body you can trigger and control the wah effect. The Soul Kiss is about the size of a pack of cigarettes and its controls consist of a high/low switch and a variable Q (frequency range) knob.

The controls you may perhaps encounter on different models are as follows:

- **Range:** this sets the frequency range of the filter from when it opens to when it closes (the top and bottom frequencies of the wah-type effect). It can take the form of a single knob or a switch with fixed high and low positions.

DOD FX25 Envelope Filter

- **Sensitivity** – This controls when the envelope is triggered according to the dynamics of your playing. Low settings mean you have to hit the note hard to open the envelope. High settings mean delicate and soft strokes can open it and keep it open easily.

- **Drive/Boost** – These are extra drives built into the filter to make it sharper and more aggressive.

- **Mode (HP, BP, LP)** – These are the options for the filter frequencies that the envelope opens – high pass, band pass and low pass. They each offer a different kind of fatness and response, and they are usually found only on more sophisticated models.

- **Gain** – This controls the level of extra gain sent to the front end of the pedal and is used to boost the guitar to push the sensitivity of the envelope, thus distorting the signal.

Some other great envelope filters that really have to be mentioned here include the Electro-Harmonix Tube Zipper, DOD's FX25 Envelope Filter, DigiTech's XSW Synth Wah, BOSS's WP-20G Wave Processor, Line 6's Filter Pro (a programmable multi-FX rack unit) and FM4 Filter Modeller (a programmable multi-FX pedal unit), Mu-Tron 3, Z-Vex's Seek Wah, Seamoon's Funk Machine, Electro-Harmonix's Y-Triggered Filter, and finally the DOD FX25B Envelope Filter.

Snarling Dogs Black Bawl

Snarling Dogs Mold Spore

4 MODULATION: CHORUS, FLANGER AND PHASER

Modulation effects are many and varied. In this chapter, we're going to look at flangers, phasers and chorus units, plus their many offshoots. These effects were more or less born in the psychedelic era of the '60s to swoosh and swirl with the hippies, but they were soon adopted in different music genres as trademark and key guitar sounds by many bands. With modulation, slow speeds with high depth settings create wide, spacious, lush sounds, while faster speeds create more crazy and wild experiences. The key is to use your ears and experiment. It's handy to note down settings or mark them on the pedal's case with a chinagraph (wax) pencil if you achieve a result that you're particularly pleased with.

Chorus

Chorus is probably one of the most basic effects in the modulation camp. Essentially it's a small delay of the signal at a constantly changing time. Because the time varies, the delayed signal's pitch changes. By moving the time back and forth, you hear a sound that goes slightly in and out of tune. When added to the original sound, it sounds like two instruments are playing the same piece tightly together. Chorus, flanger and phaser effects all use low-frequency oscillators (LFOs) to produce their rich, swirling effects. When you change their speed and depth settings, you're actually controlling the frequency and amplitude of the LFO.

Chorus units sometimes give you the choice of using different waveforms to modulate the split sound source. The shape of the waveform defines how it will move in and out of tune – for example, the triangle waveform is good for slow, shallow chorus settings, while the sine waveform works well for faster, deeper settings.

Chorus was a very popular sound in the '80s with players such as Andy Summers – check out his guitar work on The Police's 'Walking On The Moon'. It's extensively used by Ritchie Sambora on many of Bon Jovi's rock ballads, while Phil Collen of Def Leppard also put the effect to much use. U2's The Edge has used chorus a lot in the past for lush, melodic clean sounds in conjunction with different delays, while funky clean guitarists such as Nile Rogers of Chic use it to fatten, sweeten and bring crispness to their playing, both live and in the studio.

In some cases you may come across dual, quad or octal chorus. Dual chorus creates two different-pitched voices as well as the original, while the quad produces four and the octal produces eight. A stereo chorus will split the original sound and the pitched voice to two separate outputs for recording in stereo, or if you want to use two amps simultaneously when playing live.

From the hundreds of choruses available, a few that we must mention here include the Ibanez CS9 Stereo Chorus; Danelectro Cool Cat; BOSS CH-1 Super Chorus, CE-3 Chorus and CE-1 Chorus Ensemble; Electro-Harmonix Clone Theory, Memory Man and Small Clone; DOD FX64 Ice Box; Trace Elliot Quad Chorus; DigiTech XMC Multi Chorus; Visual Sound H$_2$O; and the Electro-Harmonix Stereo Poly Chorus.

Dimension is a more subtle chorus effect which became an industry standard for double-track effects. It's a spatial device that adds thickness and depth to make the guitar sound more three-dimensional, with a natural spacious feel. It uses two separate delay lines working off the same oscillator, panned to stereo outputs in order to create a super-wide image. Classic and vintage models include the Roland Dimension D, BOSS DC-2 Dimension C and DC-3 Digital Dimension, and the Fender Dimension 4.

The controls you may encounter when dealing with chorus units include:

- **Level** – This controls the amount of the effect that's blended into the original sound.

- **Rate/Speed** – This controls the speed (LFO) of the chorusing effect.

- **Depth** – This adjusts the intensity of the chorus effect.

High settings produce dramatic modulation, while lower settings can be used to produce a more ambient swirling effect.

- **EQ/Filter** – This is used to shape the highs and lows of the chorused tone.

- **Vibrato (Depth/Rate)** – These are variable settings similar to the chorus effect, using volume changes instead of pitch shifting. These controls are sometimes added to some chorus units to add extra dimension and more unique sounds, and can be found on the Electro-Harmonix Clone Theory and the BOSS CE-1 Chorus Ensemble.

Flanger

Flanging originated in the '70s but was rarely used, probably because engineers had to use finger pressure on the tape reels in the studio so they could slow down and speed up the tape in tiny increments to produce the effect. (The effect got its name because the part of the tape reel they pressed on is called the flange.) Since the invention of the electronic flanger, many variations on the same theme have emerged.

Depending on where you place the flanger in your effects chain, the sweep and swoosh of the effect is noticeably different. Placing it before the gain section on the amp or before a distortion/fuzz, will give it a tubular sound, much like the reflections heard inside a large cement or metal pipe. On a clean or lightly gained amp, a flanger with a slow speed setting can give a ghostly, hollow, shallow, cold feeling. With the width speed and regeneration (or *feedback*, as it's sometimes called) turned up to the half-way mark, a colourful wobble can bring memories of '60s psychedelia flooding back instantly. Turning all of the controls up to an extreme setting will produce a sound similar to sonic bathwater glugging down the plughole!

Connecting the flanger after the gained amp or distortion unit will create huge sonic swooshes similar to a jet plane landing or a giant wind howling. This can become somewhat indistinguishable when turned up too much, but used correctly on a slow sweep it can be totally awesome.

Trace Elliot Quad Chorus

Ibanez Stereo Chorus

The classic MXR flanger was used many times by Edward Van Halen, on 'Fair Warning', 'Women And Children First' and 'Unchained' on both sides of the FX chain. A more dramatic vintage box from 1977 is the Studio Quiet A/DA flanger with a larger sweep range and built-in compressor to give a huge jet-like sweep.

Most effects manufacturers have a flanger or two to choose from among their product lines. Here are a few models, both vintage and present: DOD Supersonic Stereo Flange, BOSS BF2, Electro-Harmonix Electric Mistress, Danelectro Psycho Flange, Ibanez FL-303 and FL-305 models, DigiTech XTF Turbo Flange, Danelectro Hash Browns, DOD FX75C Stereo Flanger.

Controls

Here's a rough guide to the meaning behind the controls you may encounter on different makes of flangers.

- **Level** – This controls the amount of effect blended into the original guitar sound.

- **Speed** – This parameter controls the (LFO) speed of the effect.

- **Depth** – Controls the intensity of the flanging. High settings of depth combined with high settings of feedback/regeneration will produce dramatic synth-like textures.

- **Feedback/Regeneration** – Controls how much of the flanged signal is fed back to the input of the module. This parameter is what gives flangers their distinctive voice. Flangers are capable of both positive and negative feedback loops, so experiment to see what suits you best.

- **Waveform** – Selects which waveform the speed (LFO) follows. Usually sine wave and triangle wave are used. Sine wave is the most easily recognised, but the triangle has a smooth response.

Phaser

Phasing – or phase shifting, as it is sometimes called – is a classic effect from the '70s that uses phase cancellation to create a warm sweeping effect. Somewhat thicker and rounder than flange, the effect is created by making an electronic copy of the original signal and moving it in and

DOD FX22 Vibro Thang

out of phase while mixing it back in. As it moves around, different frequencies are cancelled out, creating a smooth curling sound. Some models include a feedback control that sends the shifting signal back into the phaser's input module, which intensifies the sound even more.

A classic simple phaser – and relatively subtle compared to some – is the MXR Phase 90. Having only one knob to control the speed, it produces a range of sounds from an organic swirl right up to a wobbly waterpool effect. Well-known users include Edward Van

BOSS Super Phaser PH-2

Halen (listen to his first two LPs), Steve Jones (*Never Mind The Bollocks*) and Jimmy Page, on *Physical Graffiti*.

Like most modulation effects, phasers have different waveform settings that produce different degrees of smoothness – usually sine wave, square wave and triangle wave. They are also rated in stages of phase shifting. The average is around 12–16 stages, so the more stages you get, the more extreme it goes! The placement rule in the pedal/amp chain applies in the same way as for flanger and chorus boxes.

On a clean or lightly gained amp, phasers on slow settings can achieve very mellow 'swampadelic' country sounds. With the rate/speed and depth turned up they can produce a gurgling wobble, creating a lively melodic hook to many songs.

Some phasers have two units put together to provide extra depth and sweep and more unique sounds, and these are called *dual phasers*. Stereo phasers are also available, and on these devices the original signal and the phased signal are split left and right, thus creating a stereo image.

The number of controls you'll find on various models of phaser will vary from only one speed knob to a whole array of adjustable parameters, including the following:

- **Rate/Speed** – Controls the speed of the phase shifting (LFO)

- **Depth** – Controls the intensity of the phasing effect. High settings of depth with high settings of feedback produce dramatic synth-like sounds.

- **Feedback** – Controls how much of the phased signal is fed back to the input of the module. The feedback is what gives the phaser its distinctive resonating sound.

- **Resonance** – Allows not only more emphatic phase effects, but also harsh wah like tonal changes.

- **Waveform** – Selects which waveform the rate/speed follows (usually sine wave or triangle wave for different textures).

Danelectro Psycho Flange

A few phasers both vintage and present include: MXR Phase 90 and 100; Mu-Tron Bi Phase; BOSS PH2 Super Phaser and PH3 Phase Shifter; Uni-Vibe; Electro-Harmonix Small Stone; Univox Micro Fazer; Ibanez Phase Tone; Maesto Mini Phase; DOD FX 20 Stereo Phaser; Danelectro Pepperoni; DigiTech XHP Hyper Phase; and Carl Martin Two Faze.

Electro-Harmonix Small Stone Phase Shifter

5 PITCH SHIFTERS, OCTAVE DIVIDERS AND DETUNERS

Some of the most radical sounds you hear from effects pedals are produced by the pitch and tuning family of octave dividers, pitch shifters, detuners and harmonising devices.

An octave divider – or octaver, as it is also known – is an effect that copies the original signal from the guitar and reproduces it at the same time, creating two or three pitch-altered notes. Usually it produced notes one octave above, one octave below and two octaves below the original note. These notes can then be separately blended into the original to create thick bottom end, or high-end 12-string effects. Rockers such as Billy Corgan from Smashing Pumpkins – and us FX nuts, your humble authors – couldn't live without one.

One of the most (in)famous octave pedals, due to its simplicity and distinctive sound, is the BOSS OC-2. On older octavers, the tracking and reproduction of the original note wasn't as tight and precise as it is today, so they created a more sluggish and messy sound – representative of rock and '70s doom-metal bands – as they struggled to keep up with the incoming signal.

Using octave pedals helps to achieve the effect of tuning down the guitar without having to change anything, and also can create the illusion of another guitar or bass following your riff at exactly the same time. The general rule is: single notes only, please. Chords create too many notes that don't harmonise together, ending up in an out-of-tune rumble! Octaver effects can be real fun as they can make a trio sound like a quartet without the extra gear and arguing!

Some examples of the many models of octaver available are: Pearl OC-7 Octaver; Electro-Harmonix Octave Multiplexer; BOSS OC-2 Octave and OC-20G Poly Octave; Colorsound Octivider; Danelectro Chilli Dog; MXR Blue Box and Jimi Hendrix Octave Fuzz; Danelectro French Toast.

The various parameter controls vary from make to make but are generally quite simple and easy to understand.

- **Direct Level (or Blend/Normal)** – The amount of the original sound that is added or taken away.

- **Octave 1 (or Upper Octave/High Filter)** – One octave up from the original note.

- **Octave 2 (or 1 Octave Down/Bass Filter)** – One octave down form the original note.

- **Octave 3 (or 2 Octave down/Bass Filter With Sub)** – Two octaves down from the original note.

Pitch Shift

Pitch shifters are similar to octavers but are more intelligent and advanced, shifting the original note not only by octaves but by other intervals as well. Most pitch shifters work in semitones and, depending on how advanced they are, offer plenty of parameter controls for you to play with.

A pitch shifter enables you to move sound from one pitch to another, with the option of adding the original note if desired. It achieves this by recording a small part of the original sound and then playing it back either faster (to raise the pitch) or slower (to lower the pitch). It does this over and over again to create a new pitch.

You can use different note intervals to produce fantastic harmonies similar to slide guitar or dual solo lines akin to The Eagles' 'Hotel California', many Thin Lizzy tracks and many of the solo sounds produced by Steve Vai. The solo on 'Owner Of A Lonely Heart' by Yes uses an early pitch shifter.

Fantastic, weighty guitar textures can be created by pitching the original sound up and down a fifth (seven semitones), single-note pitch-shifted solos are fast and furious, and you can also use the effect to create complex new chords out of simple ones – for example, a basic Cmaj chord can be made to sound like a Cmaj9, or a Cmin7 can become a Cmin11. Guitarists often use this setting a fifth down to play fast metal power fifth passages with one-finger fretting instead of the two-finger box shape. Why do the hard work when there's a pedal to do it for you? That's what's called musical delegation! Similarly, if you

Jimi Hendrix Octave Fuzz

Pearl Octaver

MXR Blue Box

Voodoo Lab Proctavia

BOSS OC-2 Octave

BOSS Harmonist

try playing thirds up and down, crazy country and outer-space harmonies will pollute the airwaves.

BOSS manufactures the most comprehensive range of pitch shifters, including the PS-2 Digital Pitch Shifter/Delay, PS-3 Digital Pitch Shifter/Delay, PS-5 Super Shifter and HR-2 Harmonist.

Harmonist

The Harmonist is a highly evolved pitch shifter utilising 'smart processing' to detect precisely the original pitch of the signal and shift it to match a selected key. Two harmony voices can be set independently in a range of three to six semitones, or an octave below the input note.

This pedal is very unique and fantastic for twin leads, harmony, octave effects and detuned chorus. Brian May of Queen is a big fan.

Whammy

A neo-classic and standalone effect is DigiTech's Whammy. In the music business today it almost appears that a whole load of records we listen to – from country and rock to industrial and extreme metal – are using whammy effects in some shape or form. From subtle detune and harmonising to all-out octave dives, it has to be one of the most innovative and exciting inventions in pedal technology. Tom Morello from Rage Against The Machine first brought it to public attention with his use of it on

Electro-Harmonix Octave Multiplexer

their self-titled first album – especially during the solo on 'Killing In The Name Of'.

The Whammy has a real-time pitch-shifting range of two octaves up and two octaves down that are controlled seamlessly by an expression foot pedal with a scrollable choice of ranges and directions – for example, you can choose whether you want the octave to get lower or higher when the pedal is depressed or opened and vice versa. Also, there are combinations of harmonies pre-programmed – fourths to thirds, fifths to sixths, fourths to fifths, flat thirds to thirds – and when the expression pedal is depressed or opened, these are added to the original note. Last but not least is a real-time controllable deep detune with the blend and intensity controlled by the expression pedal, adding value as it is depressed.

There are three different models for guitar: Whammy Original (red), Whammy 2 (black) and XP100 Whammy Wah (metallic red), as well as one model for bass.

Detuner

Detuners do exactly what their name implies: they copy an original note, move it slightly out of tune and then add it back to the original note. The effect is similar to chorus, but closer to pitch shifter, as it doesn't move around or swirl like chorus does. This makes the effect more like a tracking effect – more transparent and not as wide as a chorus effect. It's ideal for thickening up a rhythm-guitar track or making clean chords or arpeggios chime.

Detuners work by moving the note in percentage increments (–50 to +50 per cent) and then offsetting them with very short delay times (usually from 0–60 milliseconds). Higher detune settings produce more dissonant sounds, and higher delay-time settings produce a short slapback (roomy) delay effect. Dual detuners enable you to combine two settings of detune together to achieve a wider image. With stereo detune, adding 30–60 milliseconds of delay to the detuner's voices that are panned to one side (while not delaying the other side) will change the detuner's stereo imaging greatly.

Detuners are more common as patches (programmable effects settings) in rack units, as they are a more modern take on the old choruses and tend to use the same circuitry as pitch shifters. Examples of detune effects can be heard on latter day Van Halen tracks such as 'Judgement Day' and 'Poundcake'.

DigiTech Whammy II

DigiTech Whammy-Wah XP100

DigiTech Red Whammy

6 DELAY: LOOPING, SAMPLING, TAPE, DIGITAL AND ANALOGUE

Delay – or echo, as some people call it – makes a major contribution to the recordings we hear today. A delay produces repeating echoes of the source material at a specified interval. Delay times are measured in increments of milliseconds (short) and seconds (long). Knowing the history of delay and echo will help you to understand the terminology used and techniques of many pedals today.

Delays and echoes were originally created by tape loops constructed by engineers in studios, and then on tape-looping briefcase-sized units such as the Copycat (by Watkins), Echoplex and the Fender Electronic Echo Chamber. One of the first quality tape echoes was the Maestro EP-1, released in 1963, the first in a series of Echoplex designs distributed by the company and made by Harris-Teller in Chicago. The main feature of the tube-driven Echoplex design, indeed of many tape echoes, is a special cartridge of looped quarter-inch tape that wraps past separate record and playback heads. The position of the playback head can be moved to adjust the playback time from 60–650ms.

This design was then followed up by the EP-3, a transistor-driven unit that reduced the distortion created by tubes and contributed to many classic '70s recordings, including those made by guitarists Eddie Van Halen and Jimmy Page. A later improvement on this design was The Roland RE-101 Space Echo, Roland's first offering to the world of effects processing and still used by musicians today. Instead of having one movable playback head, this model has multiple stationary heads. Delay times are changed by switching among these heads, and then fine-tuning the delay time is performed with a motor speed control. This means that you can play back on multiple heads at the same time to get multi-tap delay effects.

Next came analogue delays such as the BOSS DM-2 that were designed to give guitarists echo capabilities while being more reliable than tape delays, and with the added advantage of having a low-power circuit that could be run on batteries. They are still much loved by guitarists today for the warm tape-like sound and distorted tones they produce. A lot of rack units digitally emulate the analogue delay because of its popularity; DOD has the FX96 Echo FX Analog Delay pedal.

These days, physical tape and analogue has been replaced by digital technology, and sampling (recording short sections of music and then playing them back) has become more accurate and easier to do. Stereo delays are used both in the studio and live to create moods, ambience or the illusion of two players playing when there's actually only one. In digital delays, the input signal is sampled and held for a user-specified amount of time (via the delay time setting), after which the sample is replayed at the output. All delays have a feedback meter (or repeat knob) that is used to send a portion of the delayed signal back to the input to be re-recorded along with any new source material.

Some great examples of well-priced workhorses that have been on the pedal boards of live players for years are the BOSS DD-3 and DD-5 Digital Delay, and the DSD-2 and DSD-3 Digital Sampler/Delay. BOSS has topped this with the new dual pedal DD-20, which houses many types of the delays, and DigiTech has recently introduced the XDD Digidelay.

Some guitar players base their whole sound on the use of delays, from their simplistic use by U2's The Edge to the complex harmonisations of Brian May. The use of delay can create everything from dreamy soundscapes to aggressive doubling and sampling.

One trick is to set the delay time to be in time with the music. On older studio units this had to be done with a calculator, dividing 60 by the tempo (beats per minute) and then dividing the answer by the desired subdivisions of beats. On most modern delay units there is now a feature called *tap it* or *tap tempo*, which enables you to tap in the speed of your desired repeats manually to the music, making it all a lot easier. With more basic delays, you must generally employ the hit-and-miss approach of picking a muted note on the beat and adjusting the Speed/Delay-Time/Tempo knob until the note repeats in time with the music.

Also available are tape simulation delays that offer the original characteristics of old tape-loop echo machines. These emulate real-life sonic features such as hiss, degradation of recorded signal, wow and flutter (the slipping of the tape on the reel and tape heads, plus tape stretching) and high-end frequencies (treble) that fade as the signal is re-recorded. These sounds were originally the downfalls and criticism of tape delay, but as so many classic recordings and musicians use them, they have a trademark sound that people still love to capture (hence the call for so many vintage reissue pedals on the market today): Hughes & Kettner has the Replex, T-Rex has the Replica Delay and Danelectro has two pedals that simulate the tone and feel of a '60s tube tape echo with quiet studio features. The Dan-Echo DDE-1 and PB & J Delay are compact designs, while the Reel Echo DTE-1 is a larger, more intricate affair. Line 6 also produces a multi-delay modeller, the DL4, which includes simulations based on the Maestro EP-1, Maestro EP-3 and Roland Space Echo, as well as a loop sampler, reverse delay, analogue delays and all permutations of digital delays. Advances in delays over the years have been quite simply staggering!

Apart from many ways of reproducing delays, there are many types of delay formations. All the major ones are covered here, along with some with brief explanations:

- **Stereo Delay** – This is when the repeats of the original note are split alternately and sent to two outputs, giving the first repeat left and then the second right, and so on, while the original guitar signal stays in the middle of the field.

  On more advanced units, the two sides of the delay can also be set at different speeds. Set one side as a fast echo and the other side as a slow delay and achieve Edge-like results or that big '80s sound solo. Stereo delays can be analogue or digital, but digital ones tend to have more complex trickery to play with.

- **Ping-Pong Delay** – An aptly named form of delay as it has two separate channels of delay, with the output of

Akai Headrush

each channel flowing into the other, going back and forth like a game of ping-pong. This can be used in mono, but for maximum madness a stereo setup is essential and is a fantastic experience. You can find this feature on the DigiTech 2120 Artist, Line 6 DL4 Delay Modeller, Rocktron Intellifex and Replifex.

- **Reverse Delay** – This is a sample of the original passage or note that you are playing turned backwards and then sent to the output of the module. By turning up the wet (effected) signal full and the dry (original) signal down, just the backwards phrase is played back, giving an incredibly psychedelic experience along the lines of 'Are You Experienced?' and 'Castles Made Of Sand' by Jimi Hendrix or 'Strawberry Fields' by The Beatles, and this effect is sometimes called *warp*. You can find this on the Danelectro Back Talk and Line 6 DL4 Delay Modeller.

- **Looping Hold (Sampling Delay)** – This is when the unit samples a note or phrase for a specified amount of

time and then plays it back in a continual loop without the signal decaying, thus leaving the player to play other parts simultaneously or to add other loops over the top. This is a modern offshoot of the old tape units. Brian May used looping tape delays back in the '70s – listen to 'Brighton Rock' on Queen's *Sheer Heart Attack* LP.

This technique can be quite a complex skill to acquire, as timing and concentration are paramount. Looping techniques are used by single players who want to clone themselves and create a 'Mini-Me' army, musically, and baffle their audiences! These are more often used live, as studios would normally use samplers, multitracking or sequencers to position phrases within a song or composition far more accurately. Check out this effect on the Akai Head Rush E1 and Line 6 DL4 Delay Modeller.

- **Analogue Delay** – As explained earlier, analogue delay is an advance on tape echo and a forerunner to digital delay. Using 'bucket brigade' electronics produces a

BOSS DD-3 Digital Delay

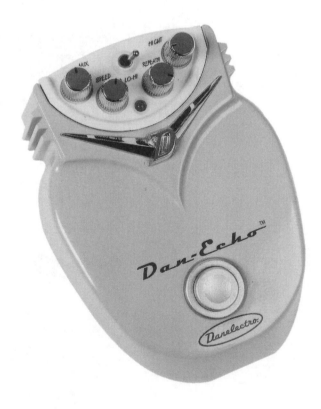

Danelectro Danecho

warmer sound, but it's not as clear and clean as digital delay. You can find it on the BOSS DM-2 Delay and Line 6 DL4 Delay Modeller.

- **Dynamic Delay/Ducking Delay** – This is when the loudness of the repeats is governed by how hard you play the guitar. While you're playing, the dynamic delay keeps the volume of the repeats down so that they don't overwhelm what you're doing. Then, when you stop playing for a moment, the volume level of the repeats increases to allow the delay to be heard. It's basically compressing the repeats down as you hit the note and then releasing when you stop. This feature can be found on the TC Electronic 2290 Dynamic Digital Delay and Line 6 DL4 Delay Modeller.

- **Modulation Delay** – A modulation delay will take the original input signal and modulate the repeats using a low-frequency oscillator (LFO). The note is sampled and repeated while the pitch is slightly changed (speeded up or slowed down), giving a chorus or detuned effect. Some modulation delay units have chorus or tremolo circuits coupled with normal delay circuits to achieve this type of effect. It's something that can be found on the Ibanez '70s Modulation Delay, Electro-Harmonix Deluxe Memory Man and Line 6 DL4 Delay Modeller.

Here are some of the controls that you may encounter on different delays:

- **Volume (or Effect/Delay Level or FX Level)** – Controls the volume of the effected signal (repeats) sent to the output of the device.

- **Feedback (or Repeats)** – Controls the number of times that the original note is repeated before it fades away.

- **Delay Time (or Length/Delay)** – Used to determine the sampling (recording) time (length) of the note or phrase you are playing.

- **Hi Cut** – A control on tape simulators used to reduce the top-end frequencies (treble) as the repeats go on. It's similar to the decaying quality of a recorded tape passing over multiple tape heads.

- **Dry Level** – The volume of the original signal.

- **Tap It (or Tap Tempo)** – A control that allows you simply to tap in the desired tempo (speed) for the repeats.

- **Smear** – Sets the spread of diffusion of the delay repeats on more advanced digital units.

- **Pan** – Used to control the stereo positioning of the original signal or the repeats.

- **Wow/Flutter** – Simulates the characteristics of tapes moving or stretching while being played on tape decks.

7 MODULATION: VOLUME, SWELL, TREMOLO, VIBRATO, ROTARY SPEAKER AND LESLIE

This chapter covers volume-related effects, which could arguably also come under the bracket of modulation as well, but to make a distinction between pitch-related modulation effects and those which change a signal's amplitude (volume), we have singled out these effects.

The most basic of volume effects are volume and swell pedals. A volume pedal is the simplest expression pedal known to man. Push down with your toe, it gets louder; push back with heel, it gets quieter. It's as simple as that, but it's great for altering the dynamics and feel of a song. 'Swelling' chords or single notes can coax violin-type effects from the guitar. Also, gain can be varied for driving the sound of the guitar for more sustain and distortion far more easily, quickly and accurately than by using the volume pot on the guitar, as on some guitars – for example, Les Pauls – this control can be difficult to access.

Many guitarists past and present use and have used volume pedals for this very reason. One example is Alex Lifeson on many Rush LPs, including *2112*. Another classic piece of guitar playing with a volume with a delay is Van Halen's 'Cathedral', from the *Diver Down* LP, although this was achieved via the guitar's volume knob and not a pedal.

For instant volume boosting at the flick of a switch for use in solos, or simply to drive the amp harder as if the pickup output of the guitar is increased, a graphic equaliser pedal can be used with the level raised. In the 1970s, Electro-Harmonix issued a pedal called the Linear Power Boost to do just this. Put before an already gained preamp, these pedals will just distort (push) the driven sound harder with virtually no increase in volume, but put it in the loop section of the amp (after the preamp) or after your distortion pedal on a clean amp and it will dramatically increase the volume of the amp – instant boosts at your command.

There are hundreds of volume pedals available, starting with cheap and reasonably priced units. The more expensive the pedal, the better the build and the more silent and clear the operation of the expression pedal will be.

Swell pedals and effects are controllable volume units that will increase the volume of the note in a time predetermined by you. They can be great for producing violin effects without all the footwork, or quick bursts without worrying about manual operation when live-pedal 'tap-dancing'. Swells are not widely popular pedals to encounter, as there isn't much demand for them, but Colorsound made one and BOSS made the SG-1 Slow Gear that performed this function with sensitivity and attack controls. It's an effect that's mostly found within multi-FX rack units.

Tremolo

Tremolo is an instantly recognisable vintage sound used not only on guitar but also on electric piano and organ. It's probably been most exploited on the guitar, and you can hear it on records through the ages, from rock 'n' roll to the most beautiful ballads of our time. As with reverb, it has been included as a stock feature on many valve amplifiers over the years. Basically, it's a signal being turned up and down (modulated) in amplitude to create a beating or pulsing effect. It's the same as turning a volume knob up and down at a selected speed, but it's being controlled by an LFO rather than manually.

As with other modulated effects, tremolo gives you a selection of waveforms the LFO can follow to produce different textures. The sine wave is probably the most common type to encounter, but the triangle waveform can become more intense and square-wave settings can create a 'gated' or interrupted sound, almost like the sound is being cut sharply on and off.

'Tremolo pan' units contain autopanners, which basically takes the beats of the note, splits them in stereo and sends them to two separate outputs, thus creating an incredibly warm, organic stereo experience both on recordings or live (with two amps placed apart from each other).

Meanwhile, the Rotovibe developed by Jim Dunlop contains a tremolo unit in which the speed can be changed

Guyatone VT 2 Vintage Tremolo

while playing by using the expression pedal (a foot pedal similar to that found on a wah-wah pedal). This can create incredible moods to suit the various passages of a song.

Tremolo effects can be heard on the Skunk Anansie *Post-Orgasmic Chill* LP (guitars by Ace, of course!) and on many LPs by Led Zeppelin and REM.

The controls you may encounter on tremolo units vary from one knob to around three. They are:

- **Rate (or Speed)** – Controls the speed (LFO) of the volume dips and peaks.

- **Depth (or Range)** – Controls the intensity of the volume changes.

- **Waveform** – Provides a choice of settings comprising sine wave, triangle wave and square wave.

Vibrato

Vibrato is an effect very close to tremolo, but it simulates the action of natural finger vibrato when bending notes using volume and speed effects. The depth is not as extreme as a tremolo unit, but the width and speed can be freely adjusted to emulate hand vibrato or the much deeper action

Jim Dunlop Tremolo

of a guitar tremolo arm (aka wangbar or whammy bar). This effect has a very '50s feel and sound and can be used for everything from sleepy lullabies to the rock 'n' roll guitars of Buddy Holly and The Stray Cats.

Vibrato controls are very similar to those found on tremolo units:

- **Rate** – Controls the speed of the effect.
- **Width** – Controls the depth, or intensity, of the effect.
- **Rise Time** – The time it takes for the effect to swell in volume.

Some examples of tremolos and vibrato from the thousands that have been made are: Colorsound Tremolo; Guyatone VT2 Vintage Tremolo; Schaller Tremolo; Electro-Harmonix The Wiggler and The Worm; Danelectro Tuna Melt and Chicken Salad Vibrato; DOD FX22 Vibrothang; BOSS VB-2 Vibrato, PN-2 Tremolo/Pan and TR-2 Tremolo; Jim Dunlop Rotovibe; Dunlop TS1 Tremolo; T-Rex Tremster; and Roger Mayer Voodoo Vibe.

Rotary Speaker

Rotary Speaker simulators – or Leslie cabinets, as they are also known – enable you to emulate the sound of an amp playing through a speaker surrounded by a rotating drum in a cabinet. Originally, Leslie Cabinets were very bulky and terrifically heavy units to carry around. Sometimes referred to as a rotary drums, a famous example is the Fender Vibratone cabinet, which can be heard on Stevie Ray Vaughan's 'Cold Shot' and is the result of a drum rotating around a ten-inch speaker. The drum has two slots and rotates in a vertical motion, throwing out the sounds in all directions.

Another version of this idea is the Leslie 145 cabinet, which contains a drum enclosing a 12-inch speaker and a spinning horn in the top of the cabinet.

The Leslie was originally invented for the Hammond B3 organ, which has a classic three-dimensional swirl and gurgle that you can hear on records such as The Beatles' 'Let It Be' and Procol Harum's 'A Whiter Shade Of Pale'. Its trademark sound is created by the time it takes to get

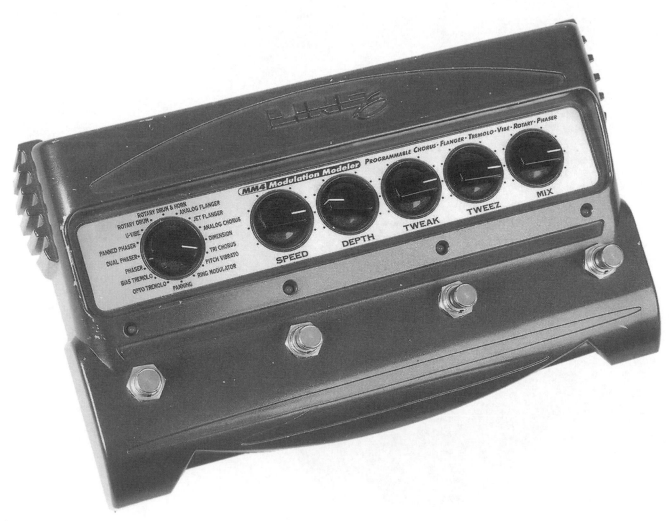

Line 6 MM4

the speaker to reach its desired speed, which creates an accelerating swell. Today, rotary-speaker- and Leslie-emulating effects are still quite rare compared to others in the stomp-box brigade.

A unique parameter in rotating-speaker simulation units is the acceleration parameter, which emulates the time that it takes to get the speaker up and running at full speed. Some units can be very complex in their huge number of parameters, as they can cover multiple aspects of the cabinet, speaker and horn. There are a number of pedal versions currently available, including the Tube Rotosphere from Hughes & Kettner. Rack units tend to have this more complex effect, and one such unit is the DigiTech 2120 Artist Valve guitar system. Another modern unit containing both the Leslie 145 and the Fender Vibratone sound is the Line 6 MM4 Modulation Modeller.

Jim Dunlop Rotovibe

Danelectro also makes a mini-pedal called the Rocky Road Spinning Speaker.

Leslie and Rotary effects can be used on the guitar to create warm, organic beds for chords, or lush, rounded notes on arpeggios. At other times the guitar can actually be made to sound like an organ, and 'Little Wing' by Jimi Hendrix is a great example of rotary-speaker effects applied to guitar.

The controls on rotary effects can be as simple as speed and depth, ranging right up to incredibly detailed fine-tuning parameters. Here are some parameters you may encounter:

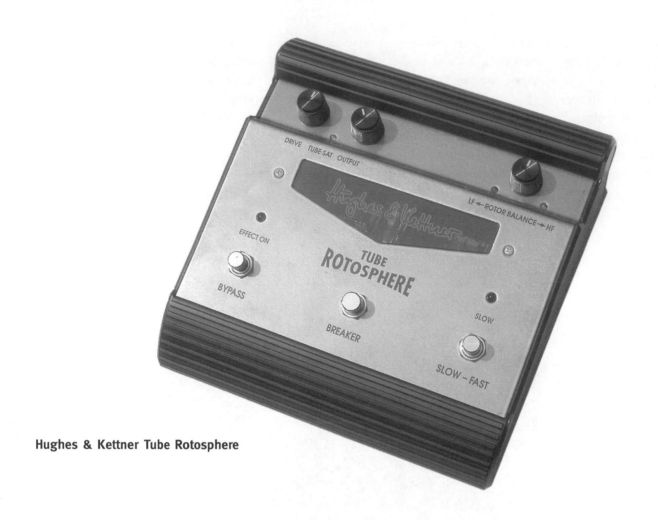

Hughes & Kettner Tube Rotosphere

Ernie Ball Volume Pedal

- **FX Level** – Controls the amount of the effect fed into the module.

- **Dry Level** – Controls the level of the dry signal.

- **Mode** – Selects which speed mode the rotor and horn are in. Settings are from fast to slow.

- **Speed** – On simpler units, this varies the speed of the drum and horn rotation.

- **Spread** – Sets the horn stereo microphone spread.

- **Horn Level** – Controls the horn's overall output level.

- **Rotor Level** – Controls the overall output level of the rotor.

- **Horn Speed** – Controls the speed (LFO) of the horn.

- **Horn Depth** – Controls the intensity of the horn.

- **Horn Doppler** – Sets the amount of shifted pitch heard in the horn.

- **Rotor Speed** – Controls the speed of the rotary drum.

- **Rotor Depth** – Controls the intensity of the rotating effect.

- **Brake** – Controls the deceleration of the rotor.

- **X-Over** – Selects the frequency at which the signal is split between the horn and rotor – in other words, which part of the overall sound is handled by each component relating to the EQ. For example, low frequencies by the rotor and higher frequencies by the horn.

- **Acceleration** – Controls the amount of time that the rotor and horn take to reach their full rotating speed.

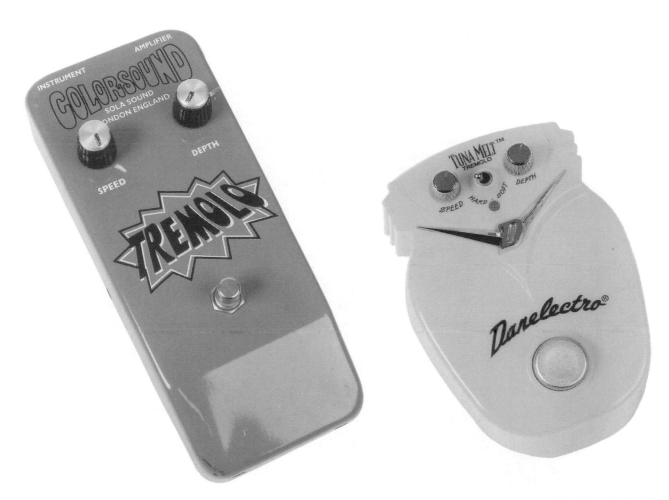

Colorsound Tremolo

Danelectro Tuna Melt

8 MULTI-FX: PEDAL, RACK AND FLOOR UNITS

Multi-FX units vary in their selection of combinations of effects, usually down to budget or size, but all of the effects that are covered in this book can be found on multi-FX units in some shape or form.

Here, the pros and cons of multi-FX units are fully explained. Some players are pedal purists and despise rack units while others have no desire to use the seemingly Stone Age technology of pedals. The authors embrace both of them to handle different duties, and indeed most sensible guitarists think this way rather than closing the door on the possibilities of using two types of technology simultaneously. A few years ago stomp boxes couldn't get arrested and were in the bargain second-hand bin at the local music store as all the shiny racks had guitarists salivating and praying for payday. These days, things seem to have swung back the other way and the racks are now the more dusty counterpart in the stores. I think that one of the reasons that pedals are so popular now is that the

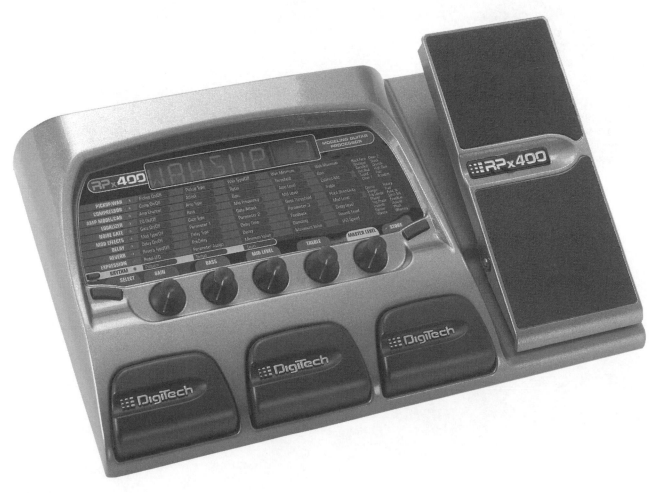

DigiTech RPX400

build quality, simplicity and uniqueness of sound from one manufacturer to another are very gratifying to experience. Now, it seems, rack multi-FX are being styled into large pedals to appear more user-friendly and cool.

Rack multi-FX units and floor units work in a slightly different way from pedals: you have to program the sounds into them rather than just indiscriminately twiddle a knob on the floor. They usually use a MIDI pedal board that is powered and controlled by the unit, with the electronics built into the pedal board.

The advantage of multi-FX units is that you can assign more than one sound to a single footswitch so that they all turn on together when activated.

The terminology is different, too, as we are dealing with virtual pedals instead of physical boxes. A programmed effect or combination of effects is assigned to one switch, commonly called a 'patch' or 'program'. Because multi-FX units are capable of many different variations and combinations, they can store many patches, from as few as four to as many as 200 and upwards. With most MIDI

pedal boards having about ten switches and most floor units about five to ten, there are more patches available than footswitches. This means that the patches are stored virtually in *banks* – groups of effects patches that are assigned to the footswitches when they are selected. So, if you have ten footswitches on your board, a bank commonly will contain ten patches that will change when you select that particular bank. Each patch may contain one effect – say, a phaser setting – or may have a combination of five or more – for example, fuzz, phaser, delay, octave and noise gate all at the same time. The more complex (and expensive, in most cases) the rack, the more effects you can use simultaneously on one patch.

Here's where it gets a bit more complex. Each patch has to be programmed to your taste if you don't like the (usually unconvincing) factory presets. Because the unit houses many effects with different parameters (settings), there is a universal set of keys, and sometimes knobs, to control and set them. Many units also have a *scroll wheel* or *navigation wheel* that scrolls through the parameters and so forth as

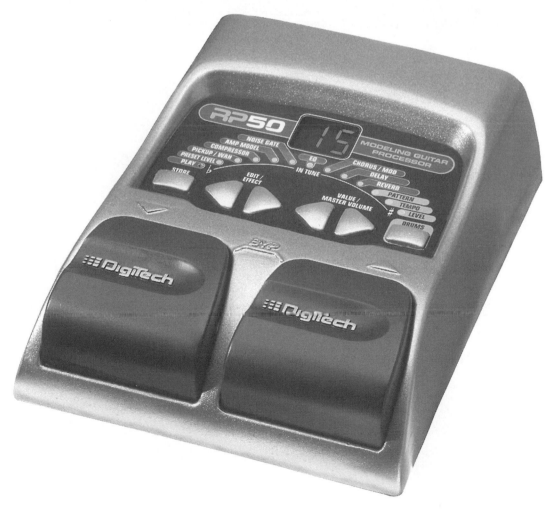

DigiTech RP50

you turn it. In other cases, it appears as a set of arrow-style up and down keys.

The word *page* refers here to any screen containing a selection of parameters within an effect. It's kind of like imagining a printed page, where each block of type is an instruction for programming an effect (ie a parameter). Basically, you scroll through the pages to find the parameters you need to change in order to shape the effect's sound. Once you've created a sound with one effect, you can store it and assign it to a footswitch or a patch on your pedal board, or you can add other effects by repeating the same process and chaining them together to work simultaneously. This can then be assigned (ie sent) to a single footswitch so you don't have to engage in pedal tap-dancing onstage when

more than one effect is required to make up the sound. Effect chaining, assigning, scrolling, programming, pages and even the terminology of parameters varies on different units, but they are universally similar in their operation and navigation.

Although the manufacturers won't admit it, some rack and floor units have problems processing large amounts of data at the same time when dealing with complex patches of combinations of effects, and this can cause a 'drop-out' when switching around between patches, manifested as either a dip in overall volume or a delay in the new effected sound appearing. This can cause problems with your dynamics and accuracy when changing to another section of a song where tightness is of paramount importance – particularly in rock and metal – and is also totally unacceptable in the studio.

DigiTech 2120 Valve Guitar System

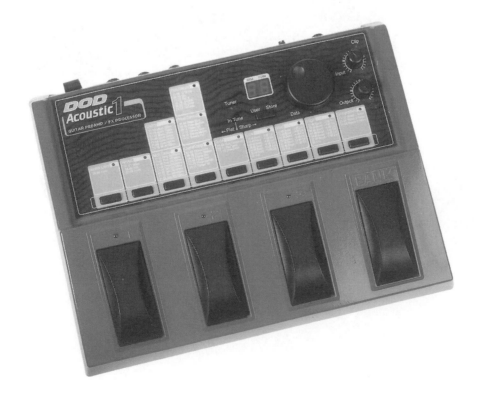

DOD Acoustic1

The only way around it in the studio is to 'drop in' to the track as an overdub when the patch is already turned on, thus limiting your prospects of achieving a one-off live take.

Racks that don't have these dips or drop-outs claim to be *seamless*, meaning that the changes are smooth and inaudible. Always check that this is the case – and still test it out to see for yourself, as the authors and many others have been burnt because of this in the past. Non-seamless rack patches are frustrating and ultimately affect your playing because you're having to work around them all the time!

Lastly, people complain about rack units changing the tone of their guitar because of all those electronics. Some units claim not to affect the direct signal that passes through them, but always check this by ear for yourself.

A way of remedying this rather inconvenient problem is to choose a unit that says it has a *true bypass*, which means that, when the effect is switched out, the guitar bypasses all the internal effect circuitry and just passes through the input and output stage.

To get the original tone within all patches is a matter of accessing the global (overall) EQ for the unit and painstakingly matching an empty patch with the sound of the bypassed unit when your guitar is plugged straight into the amp. When the empty patch sounds the same as the bypassed sound, you can then add effects and the result will be similar to that of a pedal – another possibility that manufacturers don't own up to!

Rack And Floor Pros And Cons

Here, then, are some of the benefits and disadvantages of rack and floor multi-FX.

Pros

- They do away with having to cart around stacks of patch leads, awkward power supplies and bulky, heavy pedal boards.

- Ultra-fast set up time! No more batteries!

- More than one effect can be used simultaneously, and you can switch between effects by using single footswitches.

- More accurate settings can be achieved and restored instantly without any fiddling around with separate pedals and knobs.

- They can work out cheaper than the same number of pedals for sounds.

- There is also less line signal loss than using a chain of pedals.

- They are a lot lighter and easier to transport, plus glowing lights look cool. But beware – they can be fragile and can't take a knock or be dropped, which can happen a lot when touring.

Cons

- On the other hand, they may be non-seamless and have dips or drop outs between patch switching.

- In some cases, they may thin the original tone and process the original signal of your guitar a little unnaturally.

- You are limited to one manufacturer's effects and some may not be exactly what you desire.

- Finally, with multi-FX units, all your eggs are in one basket, which is scary prospect when playing live shows and touring in case anything goes wrong with it – you will need backup!

DigiTech RP14

Pedal Pros And Cons

Now here are the pros and cons of pedal effects units:

Pros

- They are very simple to use and physically have knobs on them to control the parameters. So, when you're a self-taught, not very technical feel player, you can turn the knobs, hear the result and see the setting in front of you.

- What's more, it's easy to remember where to turn the knobs to get to a rough approximation of the settings that you use regularly.

- You can physically stamp on them! And when you're on a dark stage, jumping around, it's a lot easier to stamp on a big yellow box than, say, flick the third switch from the left second row down!

- Another big plus point for pedals is that all the components in the box are dedicated to creating one effect, and therefore they are usually more intense and diverse, as multi-FX units use one complex circuit for all of the different groups of effects. So, for example, you may like the sound of a BOSS delay, but not the chorus, and prefer an Electro-Harmonix vintage pedal. With pedal chains you can combine different makes and ages of pedals to suit the sound you want from that specific effect. Then it's quite a simple and organic process to find combinations of sounds that work together by just sitting on the floor and twiddling while you play. I use a chinagraph (wax) pencil to mark positions around the knobs for settings I regularly go back to.

- They are also very robust and can take a knock and are dropped every now and then, and they tour very well, travelling in flight cases and bags in trucks and on planes. You can save up and buy a new one every now and then, and they can be picked up second hand relatively cheaply. They last for years and years. Some of the ones that we use are over 30 years old! Hey, they look good too – there's a reason!

Cons

And on the downside...

- Pedals can be noisy!

- They also require lots of weird power supplies, tons of batteries and heavy, bulky pedal boards.

- It can also work out very expensive to get as many sounds as you get on a multi-FX unit. The more pedals, the more line-signal loss from your guitar before it reaches the amp, and the result is a dulling of the tone.

- Finally, having to do the Fred Astaire pedal tap-dance when changing to a section that requires more than one effect change at one time is a right pain!

- Also, it's difficult to reset a pedal accurately on a dark stage – and, of course, you may need to go through the resetting process between every song.

- The last point against pedals that we can think of is that setting them up if you don't own a pedal board is a bit of a pain...

Types Of Multi-FX

There are many types and makes of multi-FX, but here's a selection of some of the better-known makes that are quite easy to find:

- **Rack units:** DigiTech 2120 Artist; Rocktron Intellifex, Multivalve; Rocktron Replifex; Rocktron Voodoo Valve; Line 6 Echo Pro, Line 6 Mod Pro, Line 6 Filter Pro; TC Electronic G-Force; TC Electronic G–Major; Zoom RFX-2000; Gibson Echoplex; Lexicon MPX G2; Alesis Quadraverb; BOSS SE-70, SX-70, GX-70; Roland GP-8; Yamaha FX770; Lexicon MPX1, MPX500.

- **Floor units with large pedal board and 6–12 footswitches:** – Zoom GFX-8; BOSS GT-3, GT-5 and GT-6.; DigiTech GNX3, RP6, RP7, RP12 and RP20; Korg AX1500G.

- **Floor units with medium pedal board and 3–6 footswitches:** DigiTech RP3, RP300 and RPx400, GNX1; BOSS ME-50; Line 6 DM4 (Distortion), MM4 (Modulation), FM4 (Filter), and DL4 (Delay); BOSS BE-5M, BE-5, BE-5B, ME-5, ME-6, ME-6B, ME-8, ME-10, ME-30 and ME-33.

- **Stomp-box-size multi-FX units with two footswitches:** Zoom GFX-707, 707II, 708II (bass), 606, and 607 (bass); DigiTech RP50, RP100 and BP50 (bass); Zoom 505II and 506II (bass).

9 WEIRD AND WONDERFUL EFFECTS

In this chapter we'll try to cover a few of the more bizarre effects developed over the years that we've missed out of the other chapters so far. As there are literally hundreds of these stand-alone mutations all over the world, it would be impossible to cover them all – some of them have counterparts that are in the same ballpark, but with slightly different variations on the same theme – so, let's take a deep breath and try to cover the bulk of them with these examples. Here goes...

Acoustic Simulation

Acoustic simulation is a quite recent invention compared to most effects, and it comes in really handy for single guitarists in bands. The AC-2 Acoustic Simulator from BOSS,

BOSS AC-2 Acoustic Simulator

for example, makes an electric guitar sound like an acoustic. It has four modes for simulating different kinds of acoustic and electro-acoustic guitars, as well as fine-tuning knobs to control the simulation of guitar-body resonance, picking attack and harmonics. On a clean electric guitar, this effect can sound very convincing and is perfect for live situations when you're trying to recreate a recording where you've switched between guitars, or you want to give the impression of acoustic guitars in the composition.

Tone Shifting

Tone-shifting pedals could be one of the best-kept secrets in rock 'n' roll! The Snarling Dogs VeryTone pedal can add that lost inch of tone that you couldn't squeeze out of the classic amp sound that you searched for. Very subtle and almost transparent at times, it can give that twang or richness that is sometimes seemingly impossible to obtain. Extremely simple to use – and a quite unique freak – the VeryTone enables you to add EQ to your signal by clicking a rotary knob to different settings. 'Bite' is the name for the four-setting tone selector, and 'snarl' is the volume compensation. These types of pedals are very few and far between.

Talk Box

Vintage Talk boxes are the ideal thing if you feel like sticking a horrible tube in your mouth and guitar cables in all the wrong places, and transporting a box that sometimes weighs more than the rest of all your other effects put together (such as the Hielsound Talkbox). A bit of a one-trick pony, it gives you exactly what you want with one setting. But then again, it is as inventive as you want it to be, seeing as you shape it with your voice.

Basically, a talk box gives you the Bon Jovi 'Living On A Prayer' or Peter Frampton 'Show Me The Way' voice-guitar sound. You plug it in between your amp and cab and shape the sound (which comes up a long tube from a tiny speaker in the box) with your mouth and voice back into the microphone to the PA. It's quite an involved affair, but my

Snarling Dogs VeryTone

advice is try before you buy, because it can be an expensive loss if you can't get on with the mouth tube. Electro-Harmonix made one called a Golden Throat in the '70s, working on the same principle.

These days, there are a couple of more user-friendly versions available. Danelectro has a model named the DTB-1 Free Speech (based on the same principle as the retro designs, but the microphone is built into the tube and plugs back into the pedal to come out of your amp instead of the PA) and DigiTech has a very advanced version called the Talker that also takes in the microphone instead of the PA, and has six factory preset programs. The Talker creates intelligible words or phrases and can actually make your guitar sound as though it's talking or singing. With settings such as NuWah, Tazmania, Talkbox and Alien, I think you can get the drift!

Ring Modulation

This is a hard subject to explain and to understand for guitarists, and it's a very sparsely used effect – mainly because it seems to change the sound of the guitar randomly without any apparent logical reasoning. Sometimes it can even be difficult to extract anything conventionally musical from it!

Ring mods can come in the form of an expression pedal or a plain box. The Gonkulator from DOD is one such box that won't suit all tastes but could make some of you fall

to your knees: a twist of the knob in the right direction can unleash ridiculous disorderly sonic pandemonium. It can transform your lead breaks into banshee howls or leave them crumbling into decrepitude.

Always unpredictable and original, this pedal has no law! All you can do, really, is experiment with ring modulators until you find something that suits you. We tend to use them when we need a totally unique and bizarre sound on a recording – usually when all other options have been exhausted. The only way to describe it is as a drunken octave-fuzz-envelope-modulation cocktail! Subtlety is the key for distinguishing notes or riffs.

Other ring modulators include the Lovetone Ring Stinger, Z-Vex Octane, Charlie Stringer's Snarling Dogs Mold Spore and the Electro-Harmonix Frequency Analyser.

Treble Boost

Treble Boosters such as the Screaming Bird and Screaming Tree from Electro-Harmonix, and the new range of BSM-HS, RM and OR treble boosters, will give you that razor-sharp edge when you need to cut through live. All they really do is increase the top-end frequencies, and they aren't often seen gracing today's pedal boards. Electro-Harmonix claims that, with their models, the high end of your sound spectrum will sparkle, allowing you to taste and feel each note. Eric Clapton used the Rangemaster treble booster for solos in the '60s, while Brian May still uses a Fryer treble booster.

On much the same theme are the Electro-Harmonix Mole and Hog's Foot Bass Boosters, which cut the highs and amplify the subharmonics, giving your instrument the depth,

DigiTech Talker

Electro-Harmonix EH-5000 Frequency Analyzer

authority and penetration of the pedals of a church pipe organ! The manufacturers also claim that their models give your guitar or amp that swamp-bottom blues sound of the Fender Jazz bass used in conjunction with an old Ampeg B15.

Sitar Swami

Meanwhile, influenced by the nu-vintage invasion, Danelectro's Sitar Swami is a bizarre and original-sounding sitar-simulator pedal that comes complete with a blues slide to increase the realism. We're not quite sure if it really does sound like a sitar, but that doesn't matter as long as you squeeze out some mega-cool sounds – that's what's important. In terms of controls, there's an EQ knob and a level-adjustment knob that makes it pierce or warble in a ghost-like fashion. This is definitely a one-off item.

Space Station

We are convinced that the XP300 Space Station from DigiTech was created by an advanced alien civilisation to bring harmony and beauty to our troubled planet. As soon as we plugged in this device, we were in love! It has 39 programs that'll warm even the coldest of hearts, including

string pads and swells to sit behind your chords (Synth), Pixellator and Ring Modulator (Alien), amazing backwards guitars and autowhammy (Warp), plus arpeggiators and resonators (Sonic). We shall run our harps through it when we are angels! One of our all-time favourites, the potential of this pedal combined with other boxes is mind-blowing!

Micro Synthesizer

Another of our all-time favourites is the Micro Synthesizer from Electro-Harmonix. A large metal box with graphic-EQ-type faders to control its parameters, the overall effect is a mixture of an octave, sub-octave and square wave combined with a filter section comprising resonance and frequency controls. The 'attack delay' fader can control the filter sweep, while the 'trigger' fader controls the octave's wave and volume (collectively called the *voice mix*). Basically, it sounds like a synthesized octaver pedal with an envelope filter on it. This is a totally versatile effect capable of producing sounds ranging from crazy, buzzy, thin spiky leads, right up to fat, moog-like synth-bass noises. It's used by everyone from Smashing Pumpkins to Skunk Anansie and AceSounds.

DOD Gonkulator

Danelectro SitarSwami

Shift Daddy

The Shift Daddy is a unique echo and pitch-shift device housed in a wah-type expression pedal. Featuring four switches on each side, you can use it to create radical pitch bends or subtle note twists. You can also dip, bend or stretch any chord or single note in what is effectively a simulation of using the tremolo arm on your guitar – which is handy, of course, if you don't have one. Plus, you get the added bonus of spring and arena reverb simulations, and slap and 'Interplanetary' echoes. It takes a while to master, but there's nothing else like it.

Ebow

An Ebow is a small hand-held unit used to simulate violin/cello string passages, or to generate infinitely sustained notes on the guitar. It works via a magnet which resonates the strings and feeds back from the guitar pickups (because they are magnets, too). This creates the vibration, which constantly moves the string as though it is being constantly picked, but without the sound or attack of continual re-picking.

Many players use Ebows subtly to form beds of string pads behind compositions, while others use them as up-front melody leads, such as The Edge on U2's 'With Or Without You' or indeed Phil Hilborne on 'Murmur' (*15th Anniversary* CD).

The operation is very simple, but it can take a while to master. Basically, you place the Ebow at the bridge over the string you want to vibrate and sustain. On the Ebow's underside are grooves which rest on the strings on each side to position it. Then, you slide it slowly towards the neck pickup. As the magnet of the Ebow and the pickup come together, the string vibrates more intensely, creating more volume. As you draw back towards the bridge, the resonance decreases and the volume drops, thus creating a swelling or 'bowing' effect similar to strings being bowed on a violin or cello.

Erogenous Moan

The Erogenous Moan is a tape reverse simulator (ie it simulates the effect of a tape-edited reversed note) in the shape of a wah-type expression pedal. Depressing the footpad causes the volume to increase (swell). At the bottom of the sweep, you notice what is almost a drop in volume, succeeded by a simulated tape-edited click. Then, as you raise the footpad, the volume is reactivated and swells again. At the top of the sweep, the same drop in volume occurs, and is followed with another simulated tape-edited click.

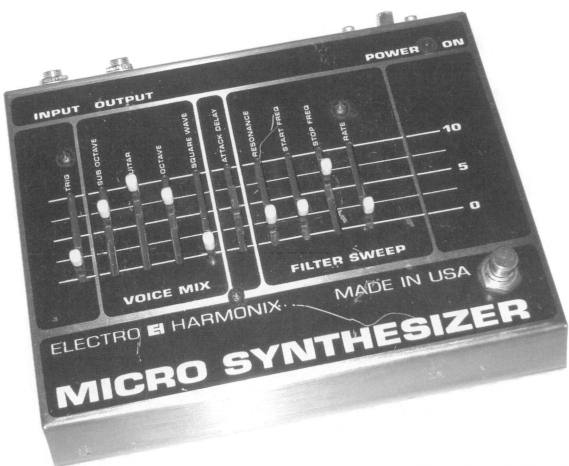

Electro-Harmonix Micro Synthesizer

DOD Buzz Box

BOSS SP-1 Spectrum

Danelectro Shift Daddy

BOSS SP-1 Spectrum

The BOSS SP-1 Spectrum is a compact pedal-style single-band parametric equaliser with two knobs for its controls. The Spectrum knob enables a continuously variable setting of a frequency of 500kHz (high) to 5kHz (low), while the Balance knob sets the sets the peak of that frequency. What all of that really means is that it's like using a wah

pedal in a fixed position of your choice within its wah spectrum (frequency range), but leaving you able to use the footswitch to turn it off and back on when you want to return to the exact setting. The SP-1 produces a similar sound to the technique used by Michael Schenker (mentioned in Chapter 3) and has attained a cult status with BOSS enthusiasts.

DigiTech XP300 Space Station

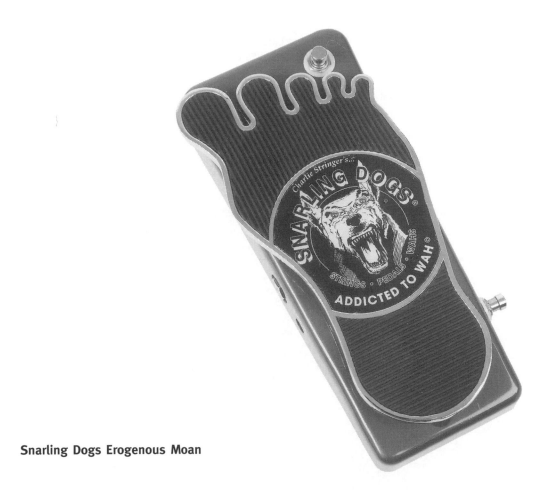

Snarling Dogs Erogenous Moan

FX33 Buzz

The FX33 buzz box from DOD looks like a metal wasp and was designed by King Buzzo from The Melvins. A crossbreed of a fuzz box with EQ and octaves, it's one of most versatile, extreme and unique pedals we own. Fiddle with the controls named 'Heavy', 'Buzz', 'Saw' and 'Thrust' and discover vitriolic, insane, thick octafuzz. At the other end of the spectrum it delivers a harsh, brittle, spiky attack capable of third-degree burns and vicious feedback. An all-time extreme classic!

Ebow

AdrenaLinn

The AdrenaLinn, from Roger Linn Design, is a guitar effects processor that incorporates a fully programmable 32-step filter, drum machine and amp modeller. With 100 ROM-based factory presets and 100 user-editable presets (initially containing the same sounds), you can combine all of these functions together to create some amazing sounds. Containing amp models such as Fender Champ, Mesa Boogie Dual Rectifier, Vox AC30 and Classic Marshall included in the 12 available, as well as a whole host of unique filter/delay effects, you can be as creative as your imagination allows, all backed up by the internal drum-machine grooves.

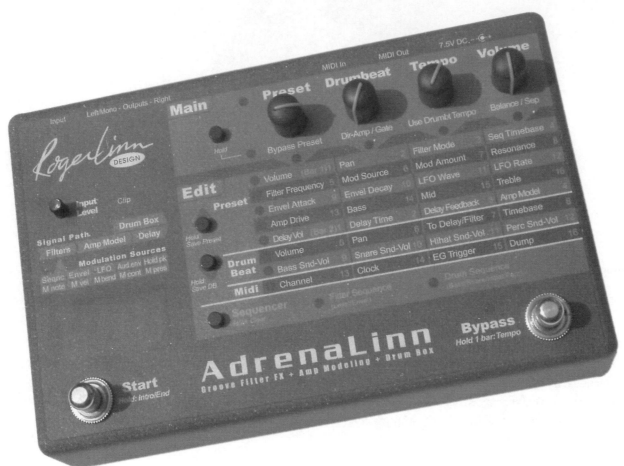

AdrenaLinn, Roger Linn Design

10 AMP SIMULATION, PLUG-INS AND VARIAX GUITAR

A very popular creative device still relatively in its infancy is amp simulation. It saves you thousands of pounds in gear, which also means a lot less equipment to cart around and maintain. What's more, vintage and rare amp models are all now available in modelling form while new, more authentic and powerful units are being introduced all the time. Some units just offer amplifier simulation while others are above and beyond this, with multi-FX and MIDI hookups for controlling patches or computer-aided remodelling.

For the uninitiated, amp simulators are basically units in rack, pedal or block form that emulate real amplifier sounds and settings for use with power amps live, and direct recording with simulated miked-up speakers. On the more budget and compact units, only replications of complete models with EQ settings may be available, while on the more complex and involved units amp heads can be matched with cabinets to your liking, thus offering endless possibilities of combinations, allowing you to create custom tones.

Another feature on some units is virtual mic positioning from the virtual cab. This can make a huge difference in the sound – as it would in a live recording situation.

Also found on units such as the Line 6 POD series is a feature called AIR (Acoustically Integrated Recording) which can be adjusted to give the impression of the spread of the sound as it passes through the air to the microphone. To be honest, the real thing is always the best, but if it sounds not quite the same but still great, an objective is achieved.

Most of the amp simulation units around use the same terminology and theory for programming and operation. Line 6's POD was one of the first to break into the market, and now we have a whole slew of followers ranging in their abilities to sound authentic and deliver quality effects.

The facilities on most units comprise a set of three EQ knobs – treble, middle and bass – plus a gain control, input volume and master volume out, while the amp models, cabinet models and effects are usually selected via rotary switches. Amp simulations and effects combinations are stored in patches, much like in a rack or multi-FX unit. Some units, such as the Line 6 POD Pro, can have a MIDI pedal board attached for live use, utilising banks for patches to the footswitches. As well as the guitar and bass POD and POD Pro units, there are also the DigiTech Genesis 1 and 3 and the Behringer V-Amp 1 and 2. All are similar in design and operation, but each has slightly different added extras.

Amp-simulator terminology utilises certain terms to describe the models of amp they are simulating. There will be no reference to particular brands of amp, for copyright reasons, so instead the terms here refer to descriptions that are copyright-free.

Here's a general key to what amp bracket we think they may be describing with their terminology.

- **Tweed** = Fender amps
- **Modern Class A** = Matchless
- **Brit Class A** = Vox
- **Brit Blues** = Marshall combo
- **Brit Classic** = Marshall Plexi
- **Brit Hi Gain** = Marshall JCM head
- **Rectified** = Mesa Boogie rectifier
- **Modern Hi Gain** = Soldano amps
- **Boutique** = Budda Twinmaster, Cornford and other small custom combos
- **Black Panel** = Blackface Fender Twin
- **California Crunch/Clean** = Mesa Boogie Mark II

Amp modelling is all in the ear of the listener when it comes to how you want it to sound. When creating a sound, our advice is to listen to some authentic recorded sounds that you like and analyse them by thinking of why they sound good, and try to identify what elements of tone, drive and EQ they contain. Then play with the simulation unit and try to recreate those nuances in the sound, and maybe compare them to the record to see what spices you're perhaps missing from the recipe.

It's all trial and error, and different guitars sound different on different amps, so maybe try to find out what guitars

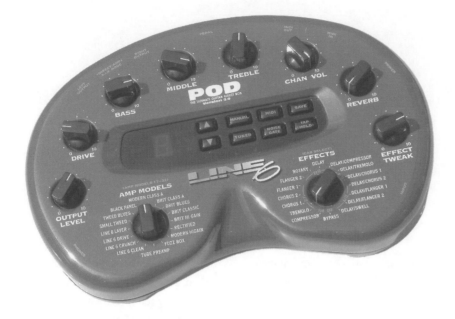

Line 6 POD

and amps were used on the sounds you're trying to capture. Once you've found a good setting, name it, store it and move on to another one. As you become more familiar with the unit and more tuned to listening to the elements that make great simulated sounds, you can always go back and tweak your initial settings slightly to bring them up to the new standard.

As with mixing, when working on an amp sound it's important to regularly rest your ears, as they will dull and tire as time goes on and will start to deceive you. Fresh ears will be more responsive to EQ and tone, so short breaks every hour or so will greatly improve your results.

We like to program a great sound in a day and then sleep on it. If it still sounds great when heard first thing in the morning, we'll leave it. Otherwise, we may just subtly tweak it to bring it into the right area.

We also always listen to the simulator through the same setup as the one we are using to listen to the records that

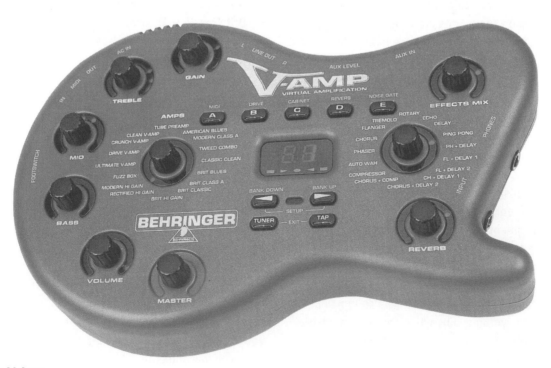

Behringer V-Amp

Line 6 Bass POD

we are initially trying to reproduce. This is because all hi-fi and speaker systems sound different, and it's very difficult to match sounds exactly if the simulator is going through a completely different setup.

When using an amp simulator with a power amp in a live situation, remember that valve amps perform differently as they are turned up – they compress naturally and become warmer and richer as the harmonics change from the driving and heating of the valves, so they will become more

pleasing on the ear. With transistor-driven amp simulation, as you turn the amp up it just reproduces the same sound, but louder. This means that you may have to tweak the EQ to avoid harshness and thinning at higher volumes.

Plug-ins

As well as the virtual amp simulation housed in physical hardware, there are amp-simulation plug-in programs available for computer recording purposes. IK Multimedia

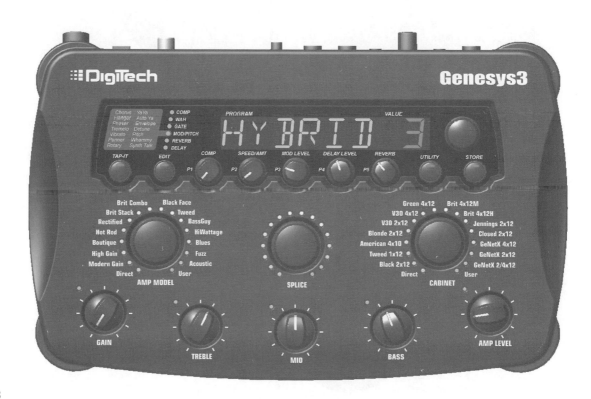

**DigiTech
Genesys 3**

AmpliTube, Hughes & Kettner Warp VST, Steinberg Warp and Line 6 Amp Farm, among others, come complete with on-screen, authentic graphic representations of the amp that you're modelling. You can 'virtually physically' turn the volume and EQ knobs with a mouse as if you were using a real amp, which is especially useful for non-technically minded guitarists with a knowledge of amps and how to achieve settings by ear.

Built-In Modelling

Along the same lines as amp-simulating units is a guitar with built-in guitar-modelling programs. The only one we know of currently is the Variax, from Line 6. In the past we've seen various electric guitars with effects built in – such as tremolo or phaser and so on – but none of these really caught on, as players preferred the quality of pedals and the ease of stepping on them rather to fiddling with the actual guitar while playing.

Along the same lines as the guitar synth, the Variax models have different types of pickups and guitar bodies, but all the electronics are housed within the guitar, removing the need for any external devices. The Variax is a solid-body electric guitar that takes the natural vibration of a string and dynamically alters it to emulate other characteristics of different guitars without the use of conventional magnetic pickups. It features tone and volume controls and a pickup selector, as with any guitar, plus a rotary selector allowing you to choose between ten different model banks, each with five sound variations of the models within their range. That's 50 different preset settings for which you can change the volume, tone and pickup positions!

Models simulated include the Martin D-28 and D-12; Guild F212; Gibson EJ 200; 1935 Dobro; 1928 National; Coral/Dano Electric Sitar; Danelectro 3021; and Gibson Mastertone banjo. Some of these models are acoustic guitars – five flat tops, two metal-bodied resonators, and a banjo.

The electric models are modelled on classic guitars with solid, semi and hollow bodies – even 12-string models are catered for! Models include the Gibson Les Paul, Les Paul Junior, ES 175, ES335, Super 400 and Firebird V; Fender Telecaster and Stratocaster; Rickenbacker 360; Gretsch 6120 and Silver Jet; and the Epiphone Casino.

The Variax also has two outputs, comprising a jack socket and an XLR plug, which can be used to send the electric models to your amp via the jack plug, while you can send the acoustic models to an acoustic amp or to the PA or a hard-disk recorder, or whatever, via the XLR output. (An A/B footswitch is also available to switch between these two sounds live.) And finally, a socket next to the jack plug has been fitted for future upgrades, so you won't go out of date.

The Variax can come in useful for guitarists playing live, as they won't have to change guitars between songs for different feels. They're also handy for studio guitarists who don't want to have to look after a stack of different guitars when they want to change textures quickly for overdubs.

Variax Guitars

11 GUITAR SYNTHESIZERS

Guitar synths are available in many different forms, from dedicated pedals to features on multi-FX units. By far the most advanced and well-known model is the VG-88 V-Guitar System from Roland.

The first real guitar synthesizer system was made in 1977 by Roland and called the GR-500. It was a large unit about the size of a suitcase and needed the GS-500 – a specially built guitar – to control it. These days, the VG-88 is a much smaller floor unit measuring about 18 x 10 inches and is considerably lighter.

The VG-88 (as used by Matt Bellamy of Muse) is an improvement on the VG-8 released in the '90s, which persuaded artists as stylistically diverse as Johnny Marr and Joni Mitchell to use it for both live and studio work. However, such a great invention came with a great price – it was over £2,000, which limited it to being a rich guitar player's tool; the average player was certainly not rushing out and buying one!

The VG-8 was a revolutionary system that offered access to many modelled amplifier and guitar sounds. As well as all these virtual electric sounds and all of the BOSS series of effects, you also had a whole range of bass and acoustic sounds that could be changed to new tunings at the touch of a button without altering anything on the guitar.

To use the VG-8 and the new improved VG-88 – which we will address now – you have to have a MIDI pickup (the GK2A) fitted to your guitar to process the sounds. This pickup can now be found built in to some new guitars from the likes of Fender, Godin and Parker, and is called 'Roland Ready', but it's still available separately, so you can customise any guitar of your choice. It connects to the VG-88 by way of a special multi-pin lead.

What makes the VG system unique, as far as guitar processors go, is the fact that each string is individually separated by the pickup and processed, which means that the sound is more detailed and versatile. The device can also retune, add distortion to and even pan individual strings! Another benefit of this system is that there is none

of the 'tracking' time, or delay, in the signal that you can encounter with other guitar synths, because the unit is actually remodelling the sound from the string to simulate the sound of another guitar. Playing actions such as slides, bends and tremolo-arm moves are all problem-free.

As well as the GK-2A pickup input to the VG-88 there are now normal guitar jack-plug pickups, which means you can independently plug the normal guitar pickup output jack in and use the effects and amp modelling on their own without using the synth-processing unit at all. As mentioned earlier, the VG-88 also contains all of the BOSS GT series of effects (distortion, modulation, delay, wah, pitch shifting and so on) and works in the same way as a multi-FX unit does – with patches, programs and banks – and you can simultaneously assign five effects at once to a single footswitch. This unit also contains an expression pedal which, in combination with the control switch, can be assigned to a number of functions within the unit, such as wah, tremolo rate, volume and reverb depth.

In a similar way to the operation of a multi-FX floor unit, patch selection is made using the up and down bank switches and the four main numbered footswitches at the bottom of the unit. There is also a large red LED patch-number display with an LCD screen underneath which shows the patch name and the editing information and bearing graphic representations of amps, guitars and speakers, making it very clear to see what the VG-88 is doing for you. The editing of programs is carried out by the use of a navigation wheel for parameter changes and via the use of soft keys (multi-functioning keys assigned to different uses depending on the page) to select values. However, if you can't face going in-depth, an 'EZ' edit function is available that enables you to change the drive tone, modulation, delay and basic sound type on one page.

As well as a built-in tuner, there is also a master volume control and an output selector switch. Selecting guitar amp disengages the speaker simulator, offering two types of output, one for a combo amp and one for a stack. Selecting

'Line/Phones' provides full speaker modelling and is the best option for recording straight into a mixing desk or recording setup.

The VG-88 uses technology called COSM (Composite Object Sound Modelling) to emulate the different amps, speakers and guitars it offers. There are 19 different basic settings, with subdivisions within them that give an endless variety of tones. The most popular is the Variable guitar. Once you've selected a basic type, there are 11 different models to choose from, which are all depicted by a graphic of the body type. After that there's a choice of pickups in any combinations you desire: LP (two passive pickups), Classic ST (three single-coil pickups) and Rick (Rickenbacker style). You can even combine the front pickup and back pickup of a Stratocaster configuration, which is obviously not possible on a conventional guitar. As well as this, you can also go into the Variable Pickup page, which enables you to customise your pickup choice as well as giving you the ability to angle the pickup to emphasise either the top or bottom strings, as well as 'virtually' place that pickup anywhere from 5–320mm from the bridge.

Acoustic guitar sounds are also covered, with piezo, microphone and magnetic-acoustic options. You can also change the size of the guitar body to emulate different tones, from flat to round or tiny to huge, as well as F-hole, metal or banjo.

The synth section contains many other emulations of all types of instruments, including brass, violin, piano, pipe, organ and orchestral swells.

Finally, the amp-modelling section contains settings for amp and speaker combinations. There are 14 amp models and 15 speaker types available for you to mix and match. Presets are modelled on classics and labelled with names such as Match Drive, SLDN Lead and Clean Twin, and these are represented by a graphic on the LCD display of your chosen amp.

Because the amp and speaker options are separate, it's possible to tailor your own sound by mixing and matching them until you find exactly what you want – for example, a matchless combo head with a 4 x 12 stack underneath it.

Meanwhile, the Editing mode works in the same way as altering the guitar types, except the controls available mimic those on the amp type being modelled. For example, if you select the VO Drive amp simulation, the virtual

Roland GR-30

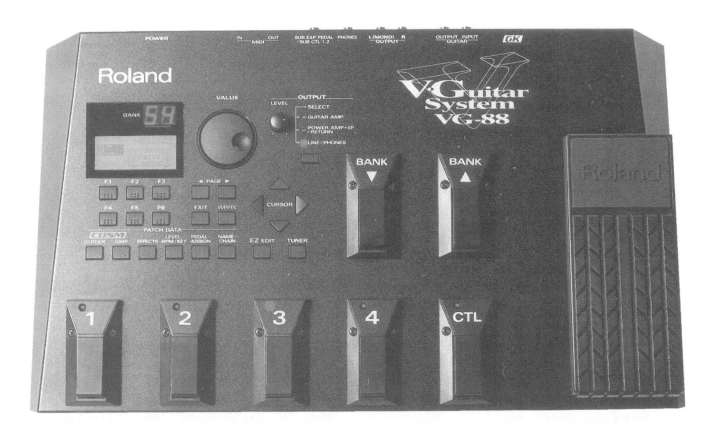

Roland VG-88 Guitar System

controls are similar to those on a Vox AC30. The speaker simulation also has virtual miking that can position the microphone 'virtually' from 1–10cm from the centre of the cone. This can make a huge difference to the tone.

In a nutshell, the VG-88 can be used as a full-blown emulating synthesizer system via the GK-2A MIDI pickup, or as a multi-FX floor unit via the standard jack output of the guitar using the standard magnetic pickups.

Here's a spec of what's in the VG-88 V-Guitar System to give you an idea of how versatile it really is:

- **Effects** – Compressor/Limiter, Wah (Auto and Pedal), EQ (four-band with parametric mids), Modulation (Harmonist, Pitch Shift, Flange, Phase, Sub EQ, 2x2 Chorus, Tremolo, Pan, Pedal Shift, Vibrato), Delay, Chorus, Reverb (Room 1, Room 2, Hall 1, Hall 2, Plate), Noise Suppressor.

- **Guitar Models** – Vari Guitar, Acoustic, Nylon Strings, Open Tune, 12 Strings, Pedal Pitch Shift, Polyphonic Distortion, Polyphonic Compressor, Polyphonic Octaver, Polyphonic Slow Gear (fade in), Bowed, Dual (Distortion and Pitch Glide), Filter Bass, Pipe, Solo, Pulse Width Modulation, Crystal, Organ, Brass.

- **Pickup Models** – LP, Classic-ST, Modern ST, Tel, Lipstick, PAF, Rick, Chet, S-S-H (single/single/humbucking), Variable.

- **Amp Models** – JC-120, Clean Twin, Match Drive, VO Drive, Blues, BG Lead, MS1959 (1), MS1959 (2), MS1959 (1 and 2), SLDN Lead, Metal 5150, Metal Drive, Acoustic Guitar.

- **Speaker Models** – Small, Middle, JC120, Twin On Mic, Twin Off Mic, Match On Mic, Match Off Mic, VO On Mic, VO Off Mic, BG Stack On Mic, BG Stack Off Mic, MS Stack On Mic, MS Stack Off Mic, Metal Stack, Acoustic.

12 NOISE GATES, COMPRESSORS, SONIC MAXIMISERS AND EXCITERS

Noise gates and noise suppressors are one of the best-kept secrets in rock 'n' roll and will soon become your best friends after only a short while of putting up with noisy effects and buzzy mains hum. Pedal chains are undoubtedly noisy, and as you add more vintage effects to your signal chain, so the hiss and buzz increases. For example, if you want to use distortion on a preamp at high volumes, you'll find that the noise between notes is pretty unbearable and distracting.

Noise gates are great in the studio for silencing hiss and interference between phrases, and for creating choppy riffs when distorted guitars are feeding back or pedal gain noise is bleeding into the sound, making for less distinction than you want in your playing. They are also useful when using clean and modulated vintage effects to fade out ringing chords gently so that they end without hiss.

Live situations are when they really come into play, though. As amps are turned up loud, chains of pedals are

BOSS NS-2 Noise Suppressor

DOD FX84 Milk Box

MXR DynaComp

the noise level you've set is reached, the gate will open in a user-defined amount of time. Fast settings will open it instantly while slow values will create a gradual swell in volume. This is used to maintain the feel of a performance and prevent it from sounding too jagged or unnatural.

In the same manner, *release* determines how quickly the gate closes after the signal falls below the threshold. In other words, when you've finished playing and the gate reaches the level of noise that it will not allow through, it will close as quickly as you have specified. Fast speeds cut the noise quickly and slower speeds will fade the signal, just as a volume control would. This value is used to fine-tune the gate to your playing and subtleties and to prevent clipping the ends off any fading notes.

On more simple pedal designs – such as the BOSS NS-2 Noise Suppressor – threshold and attenuation are combined on one knob, called 'Threshold', and attack and release are combined into a knob called 'Decay'. On a BOSS NF-1 Noise Gate, threshold and attenuation become 'Sensitivity'. A Carl Martin Noise Terminator has two channels of gating, each with a knob to control all of the settings above: one 'Soft' control, providing subtle gating for softer playing, and one 'Hard' knob, for hard gating in noisy situations. A footswitch enables you to switch between the two. It can be as simple as that sometimes!

Noise gates must always be tailored to each individual situation and player's nuances, as the nature of the noise will depend on the pedals and the circumstances and feel changes that occur during every song.

Compressors

Compression is similar in some ways to gating, at least in its operational parameters. Basically, a compressor reduces the difference between the loudest and quietest levels of an audio signal. In other words, it makes the quiet bits louder and the loud bits quieter in order to make the sound more even in volume, giving the impression of tight, punchy power or smooth, slick motion. This is known as reducing the *dynamic range* (ie differences in volume) of the signal and is a powerful tool in avoiding distortion levels and adding sustain – as well as, obviously, raising the volume during those moments of quieter playing.

Many instruments, including guitar, have a very wide dynamic range that needs to be controlled in the mix of a recording, and sometimes live, too. For tight, funky clean guitar similar to that produced by Nile Rodgers on Chic's 'Le Freak', a compressor can give an even, constant feel. In heavy metal, it can create long sustains for solos or giant-sounding power chords, and it can give riffs a wall-of-sound quality.

Compressors are often judged by their ability to control the dynamic range without creating noticeable audible side-

switched on and various mains cables creates hum, we guitarists have to silence – or at least tone down and filter out – all this unwanted noise that affects our playing and ruins the quieter moments in our songs. To this end, most rack multi-FX units have a noise gate built in to be used at the end of your effects chain.

Noise gating can be thought of as a physical gate that opens to let a signal through and closes to stop it. To set one up, you have to set the *threshold*, which is the minimum input level at which the noise gate will engage – in other words, how hard or soft you have to pick the strings to open it. Low threshold settings will open the gate and let your soft playing come through (as well as your hard playing), while high threshold settings will open the gate only when playing you're hard. High thresholds are used when there is a lot of signal noise that you want to cancel out in between actually playing.

The *attenuation* adjusts how the far the signal is lowered when the gate is closed – that is, how much noise you want to leave after the note is played. For example, if you're playing a soft piece or arpeggio, too much attenuation while gating will clip the end of the fading notes as the gate closes.

The *attack* parameter controls how quickly the gate opens when the signal reaches the threshold level. When

RockTron Hush

effects. Heavy compression can cause a signal to 'pump and breathe' with the onset of release of the compression. Some compressors can also dull the signal and lose the top end slightly. But the benefit of compression, when applied properly, is that it can add punch and excitement to instruments, as well as fatten up sounds and create a professional-sounding recording.

As well as guitars, compressors – like reverbs – are used on all instruments in the mixing process. Heavy-metal LPs these days are definitely some of the main benefactors of the compression process, from the pedals on instruments in the initial recording to mixing and then mastering (which we'll have a look at shortly).

Compressor and compressor/sustainer pedals are often avoided by guitar players because it's not always obvious what they're doing – unlike the immediately apparent effect of a fuzz or pitchshifter. Using a compressor wisely can enhance clean country leads and choppy funk rhythms, or create expansive clean chords. Studio rack compressors have a greater and more complex range of controls, while the pedal variety generally has only the bare essentials. The use of pedal compression in a live situation enables you to increase the level of your overall sound without bursting the audience's eardrums when you hit a loud chord or note.

Some of the controls you may encounter on a compressor pedal are explained here.

- **Level** – Enables you to control the amount of 'gain makeup' (the extra volume you have to add or decrease because the signal is being effectively turned down or up by the compression).

- **Attack** – Controls how fast the compressor kicks in. A fast attack gives a smooth, even envelope ideal for lush chords, while a slower one allows more of the guitar's percussive qualities to ring through before the compressor takes control.

- **Compression (or Sustain)** – Controls the amount of compression applied, sometimes specified in ratios on rack units and studio gear, such as 1:1 (no compression) or 20:1 (loads!).

- **Release** – Determines the release time of the compression – in other words, how long it takes to turn the compression off after the peak it has hit and compressed has ended.

- **Tone (or Enhance)** – This parameter adds or boosts top-end frequencies (ie treble) to the sound when some may be lost in the compression process. This helps to define single notes or the front-end attack of choppy chords.

A few examples of compressors and compressor sustainers past and present are the T-Rex Comp Nova; the BOSS CS-1, CS-2 and CS-3 Compression Sustainer; Electro-Harmonix Soul Preacher; Danelectro DJ9 Surf And Turf; DigiTech XMS Main Squeeze; DOD FX84 Milk Box; and MXR Dynacomp.

Limiting

Limiting is similar to compressing, but a limiter compresses only the signal peak (top level) without changing the sound and is designed to prevent distortion in signals that are too hot. Guitar limiters such as the BOSS LM-2 also act to balance out irregularities in the sound due to the height of the pickup pole piece and the height and thicknesses of the strings, making them good for choppy rhythm work and sharpening and defining the all-important low-end sound of a bass guitar.

Limiting pedals are few and far between, however, as the job can be handled more or less with a compressor pedal, although few examples include the BOSS LM-2 Limiter, LM-2B Bass Limiter and LMB-3 Bass Limiter Enhancer.

Mastering

Mastering involves taking the final mixes of a recording and adjusting the overall frequencies and volumes of the tracks so that they are ready to be pressed onto a CD or vinyl. For example, you may take a recording to a mastering engineer and ask him to make it sound as loud, punchy and crisp as other famous LPs. He would then adjust the bass, treble and middle frequencies (EQ) to make it sound sonically pleasing and comfortable, and bring certain instruments, such as guitars, to the fore by boosting their frequencies in the mix, if necessary.

Next, he would apply compression in order to add excitement to the mix by reducing the dynamic range slightly, giving the impression of power and volume to the individual elements of the track, as well as sinking any obtrusive or uncomfortable peaks. After this, he would limit the volume of the track by applying a limiter to stop it exceeding a certain volume on the CD (0dB). Everyone wants his or her CD to be as loud as everyone else's, if not louder, so that when it's played against another record at home or in a club, it instantly jumps out and grabs you. This is achieved by fine-tuning the compression and limiting in accordance with each other until the dynamics of the music are reduced enough to make all the elements sound loud within the track without creating distortion or making it sound unnatural.

Worth a mention in this section is the BBE Sonic Maximiser, a standalone effect rack unit (also available as a VST plug-in for computer recording) and a fantastic tool for adding clarity, warmth, bottom end and crisp highs. With this tool, acoustic guitars have a breathtakingly natural sparkle and presence while bass has more punch to the bottom end without muddying up the mid range.

Basically, when a sound goes through a speaker, the proper order is lost. The higher frequencies are delayed. A lower frequency may reach the listener's ear before or perhaps simultaneously with a higher frequency. In some cases, the fundamental sounds may be so time-shifted that they reach the listener's ear ahead of some of the harmonics. This is technically called *envelope distortion*, and we perceive this loss in sound quality as being 'muddy' and 'smeared'.

This is where the Sonic Maximiser steps in and processes the sound to correct it electronically. Its simplicity in design is amazing and it's very user-friendly: two controls and an In/Out bypass switch. Lo-contour adds and corrects the round, warm, bottom-end frequencies while Process adds and corrects the higher top-end frequencies, presence and clarity. It's as simple as that and is one of the most incredible devices for clean tones ever invented. Models include the BBE 362, BBE 462, BBE 482, BBE 882 and BBE 882i.

Exciters

Exciters are similar to the Sonic Maximiser, in that they change frequency response rather than being effects that alter the original sound. In fact, exciters basically do what the Sonic Maximiser does by simply enhancing the top and bottom frequencies, processing them and reshaping them with a transient discriminate harmonics generator. This means that, for instance, if you're playing a heavily distorted metal riff, you can add any bottom end that may be lost, and also add extra clarity. Or, if you're playing an acoustic guitar, an exciter can achieve a sweeter, less brittle sound, and control low-end thumps. Finally, on a bass it can add super low end, a pronounced mid-range bite and a meaty bark. Fretting and finger sound can be enhanced by the Hi Tune control and, with a bit of fine-tuning, finger picking on flat-wound strings can produce a great Motown sound.

Some of the exciter pedals currently available include the Big Bottom Aural Xciter range from Aphex. The Acoustic Xciter, Bass Xciter and Guitar Xciter all use the same controls – Lo Tune, Lo Blend, Hi Tune and Hi Blend – and are similar in operation to that of the BBE Sonic Maximiser. The Hi control adds top-end clarity and bite, and the Lo adds bottom-end warmth. The blend dictates how much of each enhanced signal is added to the dry sound.

13 EFFECTS LOOPS, MAINTENANCE TIPS, A/B AND SWITCHING UNITS

In this chapter, we thought we'd include a few basic offshoots from the use of effects pedals and units, such as some handy hints and tips, plus some lesser-understood simple technical uses.

One of the most frequently asked questions about effects is to do with effects loops: 'What are they used for and how do I use them?' An effect loop is normally found on the back of an amplifier and is used to insert effects pedals after the preamp section but before the output section. In other words, you can plug your guitar straight into the amp, thus not losing any signal or tone, and the effects are linked into the amp after its first section.

OK, an amp has usually three sections:

1   The preamp section, where the guitar plugs in;

2   The channel or channels to which the signal is sent, depending on your choice;

3   The output stage, where all the larger valves or transistors do their work and turn it all up.

The effects loop has two jack sockets: one send and one return. You put your pedals in order from the first to the last, and take the lead from the first pedal to the send and the lead from the last pedal to the return.

Be aware that the placement of some pedals in your chain can affect their sound. For instance, the placement of a flanger in the effects loop can produce a huge jet-plane sweep, but a subtler warble can be achieved by placing it before the preamp.

Some guitarists have their pedals located immediately before the preamp (ie straight from the guitar to the amp) while others put them in the loop. This is a more sensible method for achieving what you want, and it means that you spare yourself the problems of losing signal and tone from the guitar. In all honesty, though, getting exactly the sound you want is a process of trial and error – plugging and unplugging effects before and after the loop to see what suits you. There really are no hard-and-fast laws governing what sounds right or wrong.

Pedal And Rack Maintenance

Good treatment of your FX gear will prolong its life and hopefully not put you in a compromising position when playing live...

It's a lesson we all learn when we get our first pedal, still worth mentioning here: if you leave the guitar lead in the input jack socket on a pedal, it will drain the battery when you're not playing. The way to avoid this is either to unplug when you're finished or plug a power-supply lead into the power socket. As soon as you plug in the AC power lead, it disconnects the battery, thus saving its power. So, if you have a powered pedal setup, you can leave the jacks plugged into all of the pedals and switch the power on and off when you want. But a good tip is to leave batteries in the pedals in case you have a failure with your power supply live; then, of course, you can pull out the power leads and the batteries can take over.

Another tip is to carry out simple maintenance, such as making sure the nut around the input and output jacks is tight and secure. If it gets loose and falls off, the socket will fall inside the pedal, making it impossible to use. This applies to cabinet sockets, too. Transportation and repeated use usually cause this to occur quite frequently.

If the jack socket becomes dirty, it can create crackling noises or dull the signal. Cleaning the inside of the jack sockets with a cotton-wool bud soaked in cleaning alcohol can rectify this problem and make a noticeable difference. You can clean lead jack plugs this way, too.

A dusting or wipe-down can also benefit most pedals, as dust or dirt can cause problems for the pots in the knobs, making them crackle or drop in volume. For proper cleaning of the pots (that's any kind of rotary knob) on effects pedals and wah pedals, electrical-switch cleaner can be used. Simply spray the cleaner around the pot and turn it rapidly back and forth to work in the solution, repeating this procedure until the crackles stop. If there is no improvement, the pot will have to be replaced. This method can also be used on guitars and amps.

When using a power supply, always check its polarity, as well as that of the pedal – ie, whether or not uses positive or negative poles (the way the power input is wired). Most pedals will have the polarity written next to the AC power input, and most power supplies have it written on the case, too. Connecting the polarity the wrong way round can cause hum or non-function, and in some extreme cases it can fry the effect! And, of course, make sure that the voltage is right for the pedal before you plug it in, particularly when using combinations of UK- and USA-manufactured pedals.

Always disconnect or remove their batteries if you aren't using the pedals for a long time. Keeping them connected can drain them, too, albeit on a small scale, but over a long time this can certainly happen. Also, batteries can be prone to leaking and ruining the electronics inside, which can be very costly!

When travelling with some rack multi-FX units, it's has been known to occur that, after putting the unit through an airport X-ray machine, all the stored patches have been erased by the magnetism of the machine. It's always best to ask if it is safe and try not to put anything through unless you really have to. Let the staff check it manually, if they will oblige. Not all units are as sensitive as this, but it has

Whirlwind IMP

certainly happened to us before. Rack units are like computers, in that they store digital information that is sensitive to magnetism and the magnetic fields produced by some types of machines.

Also, when touring, try to put rack units in protective casing wherever possible. Some cases are 'sleeved', which means they have an inch or so of foam around the chassis

Morley A/B Box

that you are screwing the rack into – that is, in between the chassis and the outside case. This insulating layer absorbs the bumps and shakes caused by transit and roadies and is about as safe an environment for your gear as you can get.

If possible, always back up the data and programs from your rack units, in case of any accidents or failures. If the worst happens, you can then download everything back onto your new or fixed unit when it is returned, without having to face the horrendous task of reprogramming all of your patches. When fixing units, manufacturers tend to lose all of their stored patches and usually return them with only the standard factory user programs.

Rack care is very simple: keep units away from extreme heat and strong magnets, dust them every now and then, and don't drop them!

A/B Boxes

An A/B box is used to switch one guitar signal between two outputs – for example, two amps, one clean and one dirty. They can also be used the other way around to switch between two different guitars in order to go to one output (one amp), which saves unplugging on stage. You can use them for switching between anything – for example, effects combinations or rack units.

Switching units perform the same task but with more outputs, and can assign multiple outputs simultaneously from one source – for example, running two or three amp

rigs at the same time to create a blend of sound from a single guitar.

There are many A/B boxes and switching units available today. Some examples are the Whirlwind (Selector), DOD (AC270), Lehle (Dual, 1@3 and 3@1) and Morley (AB).

DI Boxes

A DI box is a device used when you want to plug an instrument (with an unbalanced signal out) straight into a recording desk or PA mixer (which requires a balanced signal in). It takes a standard guitar-lead quarter-inch jack into the input and then outputs via an XLR Cannon jack socket. Good-quality units have an earth lift switch that can cancel hum from the instrument level as it is converted to mic/line level. Some bass amps have DI outputs that can be used for recording or for live shows, and some amp modellers and FX racks have DI outs to record the dry signal at the same time as the effected signal. A good example of this use is the recording of a live concert.

With DI-recorded tracks, a process of 're-amping' can be used to achieve new or differently gained amp sounds at a later date. This is sometimes used during the mixing of live LPs when there's too much overspill from the band over the cabinet mics. The DI-recorded track is played out of the desk via a DI box back into the amp with the cabinet miked up. This is then recorded as a new track in a controlled environment.

DI tracks are sometimes also recorded as safety tracks.

Behringer Ultra-DI   **Electro-Harmonix Switch Blade**

14 PEDAL BOARDS

In this chapter, we'll talk about pedal boards, including setting them up and making them. Over the years, we've both had many different setups and boards to suit our needs, depending on our financial circumstances!

You can actually buy pedal boards from BOSS (BCB 6G) and Danelectro (DJ-C pedal board for mini-range) with moulded cases and a power supply included, but these are good only if you use their own pedals – and a maximum of five or six of them, at that. If you want to mix and match, you have to look a bit further or make your own. SKB Cases make a few different models with flat bases to accommodate any size of pedal and a built-in power supply, plus either a soft or hard case. J Chandler, meanwhile, manufactures a board called the Pedaltrain, which is a stepped, two-tier metal track to which you can affix pedals

and power supplies of your choice with velcro and also comes in a strong carry case.

On the whole, the majority of people tend to make their own pedal boards, especially if these are quite simple and small. Giant creations involving many pedals, power supplies, outputs and switching systems tend to be made by professional pedal-board makers such as Mike Hill, Pete Cornish or Bob Bradshaw. Rocktron makes a system on which you can have all of your pedals in rack drawers off the stage, controlled by a MIDI footswitch unit onstage.

DIY Solutions

Here are a few tips on making your own board to suit your needs and budget while maintaining reliability and ensuring easy maintenance.

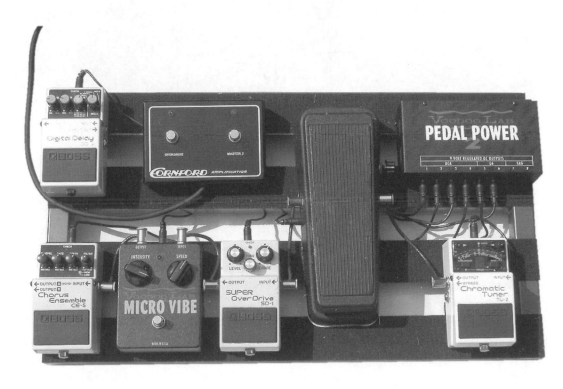

Phil Hilborne's pedal board

First of all, you have to work out how many pedals you want to include and whether you intend to expand on them in the future. Lay them all out plugged in and spaced as you prefer in order to ensure easy switching without accidentally triggering two at the same time. Now you have the basic length and width of the board.

Next, decide on the order in which they work best together, then find connector leads of the necessary length to chain them together. Remember, the shorter the lead, the less line-signal loss, so make your leads as short as possible. (This also makes the board tidier and less confusing when troubleshooting.)

It's always handy to include a mutable tuner in the board, if you have one, for quick tuning onstage. A noise suppressor or gate at the end of the chain is also handy to calm noise from all the various pedals and power supplies.

Next, you have to figure out all of the AC/DC voltages of the pedals so you can send the right power to them – and check all the connections. Most pedals are 9V and can be covered by a universal power supply distributing around 8–10 outputs via connector leads. Some input connectors vary on pedals, so make sure you have all the right terminators on the connector leads.

Choose the right regulated power supply to suit your needs. These can cost you anything from a few pounds to hundreds, depending on which make and model you choose, so shop around and ask questions. A few recommended models are the Sound LAB GO25M, Dunlop DC Power Brick and Voodoo Lab Pedal Power 2.

If you have pedals that have to use their own power supplies because of voltage differences, purchase an extension adapter plugboard fitted with an indication light

Ace's pedal board

(so that, if you're playing on a dark stage and the power to the unit fails, you'll be able to spot the problem instantly). Make sure there are enough sockets for the plugs plus one extra socket free so you can plug in the power supply, too.

The lead from this extension can then plug straight into the mains supply. If you can find a board with an on/off switch, this can be handy when you want to turn the power off to the pedals during breaks while recording or rehearsing without unplugging from the mains.

Now it's time to lay all the components out together and arrange them in a convenient and logical way, utilising all the space between them. This will dictate the width and length of your board. We tend to lay all the pedals in a line – or in two tiers, if you have that many – and then, above that, the power supply plugboard and individual power supplies are positioned to make a compact and easily manageable setup. The more organised the board is, the easier it is to troubleshoot when things go wrong.

Mike Hill pedal board, used by Johnny Buckland (Coldplay)

The base of the board can be a flat piece of wood, or it can have a gradient created by a wedge at the top underside, for angled switching. We tend to prefer tapered edges around the sides to stop the pedals from being kicked off, or the power supplies from being knocked out and damaged by touring and rough treatment. The pedal end is low (about one inch) so that the pedals can still be stepped on properly, and the power-supply top is high (about three inches) to protect it.

The next step is to go to a haberdashery store and buy

Snails Pace Slim's pedal board

a big roll of industrial-strength black velcro (hook and loop), about 2–3 inches wide and around a couple of metres in length. Now place the hook (hard) velcro in strips along the pedal area of the board and also the areas that the power supply and plug board will occupy. Lastly, affix the loop (soft) velcro covering to the bottom of all the pedals, power supply and plug board, and then stick them firmly into place.

Once you've connected the relevant power leads and patch leads to all areas, you're ready to go – with the added bonus of being able to change pedals and hookup order easily. You can even make a lid, if you desire, or perhaps fit everything into an old guitar or keyboard case. How elaborate you get on this design is ultimately up to your imagination and elbow grease!

Mike Hill pedal board

15 STUDIO RECORDING TECHNIQUES

This chapter covers the basic recording techniques for guitars, plus other elements of recording and mixing in general. Obviously, the more you experiment and the more you record, the more you will develop your own techniques and preferences for types of gear, as well as finding out what works well for you.

Monitoring

The first step to successful recording is checking the monitoring arrangements – in other words, the speaker system. Remember that your monitoring experience will differ from room to room – particularly if you were to contrast a home setup with that of a top studio. Reflections from the walls, floor and ceiling can interact with the sound produced by the speakers, highlighting some frequencies, changing the overall sound and giving a false audio impression. For instance, the room or placement of the monitors can give extra bass response or harsher top-end frequencies that you may take out with EQ, resulting in a mix that sounds wrong in a different audio environment. If you have a home recording setup, you can overcome this without spending thousands of pounds on acoustic room treatments by using what are known as nearfield monitors, which are designed to sit relatively close to your listening position. Make sure you don't place them close to the nearest walls, however, as this will prevent you from hearing the often deceiving reflection of sounds.

A professional studio will usually have two or three sets of monitors to switch between, allowing you to listen to a track on different systems with different frequency responses, such as a domestic hi-fi, a club PA or the radio. Monitoring will sound different in different studios because there are so many different manufacturers of kit, and how it's used is down to the personal tastes of the engineers who use it. Some engineers get to know the sound of their monitors so well that they even carry their own.

When you only have one set of monitors, you should try out your mixes on other equipment, such as your car stereo, ghetto blaster and domestic hi-fi system. If the mix sounds good on all of them, you've most probably achieved your objective.

Another important way of familiarising yourself with your home system is by listening to all of your favourite recorded sounds – all genres, from acoustic to heavy metal – through it. If you're using a pro studio, you should always carry your favourite CDs with you and listen to them before recording in order to pick out any differences there may be between your monitoring sound and what you're used to listening to. You should then bear this in mind and compensate by ear when you come to adjust EQ. It's also a good idea to compare your own sounds continually or mix to professional recordings that you are familiar with, taking note of tonal balance, clarity and dynamics.

Finally, but very importantly, don't have the monitors too loud all the time. Your ears will tire and lose the ability to judge the top-end frequency response. Playing the mix – or sounds for tracking – really loud can make the music seem more dynamic and exciting than it really is. You must remember that most people don't listen to records at club or gig volumes! You can eventually damage your ears as well – which is something you really don't want to happen. The solution is to give your ears a break every so often, and, if possible, sleep on your mix until the next morning, when things will sound different as you will have fresh ears. This is the time when you can give your mix the final tweaks that are necessary to bring it up to standard. Checking your mixes on headphones is also a good way to pick out any glitches or clicks that you may have missed from the nearfield monitoring. A good trick is to listen to the mix at a really low volume, or stand outside of the room to see if an instrument is too loud in the mix and popping out too prominently.

Positioning Equipment

The next step will to be finding out which room – and whereabouts in that room – makes instruments sound good. Reflections, room sizes and materials will all make a difference to the sound of an amp, drum kit or vocal. The best solution is to set up and see how things sound, then move the gear accordingly if you require a different ambience.

In addition, you can always place a condenser mic (or mics) in another part of the room to capture the difference in sound in that area, then blend it in later on. (These are referred to as *ambient mics*.) If you're recording in a studio other than your own, a good trick is to ask the house engineers where certain instruments sound the best; as they're always recording there, they will know straight away, and this can save you a hell of a lot of time during the setting-up stage.

Capturing A Vibe

As we all know, music is about feel, and us musicians are a sensitive bunch sometimes. This is why, when capturing a great vibe, setting up and making players feel comfortable is often as important as the recording itself. Obtaining as good a source sound for each instrument is very important, too, as it makes the player more confident and relaxed and prepares them to give the best performance they can without worrying about the mix. Equally important is well-balanced monitoring in the control room. Together, these elements create the vibe that will get the juices flowing and result in happy musicians interacting well with each other. A well-balanced mix at the right volume can also help the vocalist deliver a much better vocal, with more confidence and far better pitching.

Some musicians – including ourselves – prefer to track guitars in the control room with the monitors instead of over headphones. A good trick is to take your amp head with you and run a long speaker cable from it into the live room so that you can tweak it by your side and don't have to get up and go into the live room to make adjustments, ruining your flow. Also, most valve amps tend to sound better cranked up fairly high – round about the 7–8 mark, where the valves start to heat up and produce richer harmonics and a hotter sound with some pleasing, natural compression. This is known as having your amp 'wound up' or 'hot'.

Microphones

When it comes to mics, the first thing you must decide is which microphone will suit the sound that you're trying to achieve. There are two types of mic that will do the job of recording just about anything, from instruments to vocals. These two types are condenser mics and dynamic mics.

Condenser Microphones

Condenser mics are generally more sensitive than their dynamic siblings and can record lots of high-end detail.

They may also have *pads* – switches enabling them to record high-volume sources, such as a cranked-up Marshall stack, without distorting. They are generally the first choice for recording acoustic guitar and vocals, but they can also be used to get a clear, glassy tone on clean amps, or a warmer, grainy tone on distorted amps.

Most condenser mics require connection to a power supply, which is usually run at 48V and is known as *phantom power*. This power source is usually integrated into the input channel of the mixer, and the power for the mic is sent down the mic cable. There are some mics – such as the AKG C1000S – that use a battery instead, and these types of mics are known as *back-electrets*.

Dynamic Microphones

A dynamic mic is generally tougher than a condenser, doesn't require a power supply and can handle louder volumes, such as cranked amps, without any adjustment at all. A classic example is the Shure SM57, which is also used for live shows.

Because there is less extreme top end in an electric-guitar sound coming from an amp, the more delicate and expensive condenser mics tend to be not so essential. Sometimes, a condenser mic may be set back in the room to capture different nuances of the cab sound while the dynamic mic catches the up-front direct sound. These signals can then be blended to encapsulate a complete live tone.

Some engineers (including ourselves) may set up a combination of mics around the different speakers in the cab and compare them while the guitarist plays. They will then choose a blend of two and reverse the phase of one of them to capture a unique, rich texture that one mic alone could not achieve.

As well as this multiple-mics method, recording the sound from an amp can also be as simple as using one mic – such as a Shure SM57 or Sennheiser MD421 – placed directly in front of the best-sounding speaker in your amp or cab. Have a listen to them individually at a moderate volume by moving your ear around the cab while someone else plays the guitar. When you've chosen a good spot, the mic can then be placed right up against the grille or a couple of inches away.

The positioning of your mic is very important in capturing the recorded sound, so experiment by moving it around to find the best position for the tone you wish to achieve. It should be positioned at any point along the imaginary radius line that runs from the centre of the speaker cone to the edge. The various positions along this line create vast differences in tone: in the dead centre of the cone, you'll get the most bright, powerful, punchy, direct sound, and the further the mic is moved to the edge of the speaker, the darker the sound will become. The mic can be placed at right angles to the plane of the speaker or tilted at an angle of 45 degrees, creating a different tonal balance, described as being 'off axis'. (Some modelling units have this as a setting on their emulated speaker outputs.)

For bass guitar, it's common practice to take an output from the DI of the amp, if it has one. This is good for using in the mixing stage to blend with the mic sound in order to get a full frequency response from the bass, as it can be EQ'd separately.

Rather than miking amps, you could always use speaker simulators instead – or, in some cases, at the same time. (Be sure to reverse the phase of one of them.) Units such as the Sequis Motherload, the Palmer Speaker Simulator, the Marshall SE-100 and the Red Box from Hughes & Kettner can take the direct load of the amp from the speaker output and run it straight into the desk without the need for any miking. These units are great for home studios, where loud volumes or separate live rooms can create a problem for neighbours, as the amp can be wound up as loud as you want but the output is controlled on the desk, enabling you to listen at a comfortable volume.

Another useful tool in high-volume situations is a *power soak* or *power break*, which plugs in between the amp and cabinet. With this in place, the amp's master volume can be turned up high to capture a rich valve tone while the power soak determines the volume fed to the speaker cab, thus giving a driven high output at a lower volume. Marshall produce a model called the Power Brake, while THD has a range called Hot Plates.

Recording Acoustic Guitars

The miking up of acoustic guitars is another area which involves moving the mic to different positions to capture different tones. The sound tends to be more boomy nearer the soundhole but brighter and more percussive nearer the bridge. Acoustic guitars are usually miked using a condenser mic facing towards the strings and positioned a few inches away from them. Often, the best sound is obtained by placing the mic in a position somewhere between the soundhole and the 12th fret. If you want to capture more of the top or bottom strings, you can angle the mic slightly to give them more priority.

Once you've determined the best position, the golden rules to follow are:

- Make sure that belt buckles, zips and buttons are away from the guitar body, as condenser mics are very sensitive and will always pick up other sounds;

- Make sure you're in a comfortable sitting position so that you don't move around and change your position on the mic;

- Take off your shoes and place a cushion under your foot in order to muffle any foot-tapping you might unconsciously engage in while playing!

- Watch out for deep breaths and sniffing while playing.

Tracking Guitars

Once you've recorded your first guitar track, you may want to track one or several more against it. One trick is to change guitars to a different sound that might not be included in your original tone – a humbucking or single-coil guitar, for instance.

Alternatively, you could use the same guitar again but run through a different amp with a different gain setting. Cleaning up can reinforce melody and tuning, while adding more gain can add vicious abrasive harmonics and fire.

Another trick is to thin the guitar using EQ or pedals, blending this into the original, fatter rhythm-guitar part in order to give more edge and top-end bite.

When tracking the rhythm guitar, take out the original guitar track and play to the drums and bass again. This ensures that the subsequent overdubs are tight and don't waver. If you need to listen to the original guitar for reference, it's best to turn it down slightly and pan it to one side while panning your current guitar to the other side, as this allows you to remain tight with the drums and bass as well as hear the original take.

It's also vital that you tune up between every take and set up the intonation of the different guitars well. If you don't do this, you might encounter tuning problems at a later stage. Also, if you're recording a band, try to get each musician to use the same tuner or make sure that the separate tuners are calibrated identically, as some do differ.

Overdubbing

Overdubbing is an important method of adding hooks and melodies to and artistically embellishing tracks that you may not be able to perform live – and here, if you're in a live band, try not to get too carried away with the overdubs, as it may be difficult (or impossible) to recreate your material live. A few overdubs here and there, plus a bit of double-tracking, can reinforce melodies or add weight to the sound that the volume and visual aspect of a live show normally adds.

Remember, however, that the more overdubs you apply, the more tracks you have to fit into the mix at the end. Too many tracks and melodies can clutter the mix and take away from its simplicity and direct energy. Also, the mixing time will take far longer and be more complex the more overdubs you add to a song.

Noise Gating And Suppression

When recording guitars, you may encounter noise such as hissing, buzzing or electrical hum. This noise can be caused by many factors, including mains transformers, noisy pedals, electrical studio equipment and close proximity to a computer monitor, and it can increase or decrease with different types of pickups on your guitar. Single-coils can be particularly noisy, and in some cases you may be wise to change them to noise-cancelling pickups that retain a single-coil sound. These pickups are available from manufacturers such as EMG (Active), DiMarzio, Kinman, Seymour Duncan and Fender.

To locate the source of the noise, turn off all the computer monitors, although if you have to leave any on then make sure you stand well away from them. Turn through 360 degrees to find out where there is the least noise. Try to stay in this position in order to minimise the noise, and if you need extra reduction, try a noise gate such as the Drawmer DF30, a single-ended noise filter which works well for the elimination of high-end electrical buzz.

If the noise from the pedals is a bit more extreme, you can use a noise gate, but be careful: noise gates can clip or gate out fragments of sound by mistake – especially if you don't set the sensitivity correctly – thus making your guitar playing sound clipped and unnatural. On the other hand, gating heavily distorted guitars can add choppy, precise rhythms, and this technique is used by many heavy metal bands. Most of the time, serious and professional-sounding gating is left until the mixing stage, where it's easier and usually far more detailed.

Compression In Studio Recording

As explained earlier, a compressor reduces a signal's dynamic range by – simplistically speaking, of course – making the loud sounds quieter and the quiet sounds louder, and the ways of applying compression are detailed in Chapter 12.

When compression is used in the mixing process, it can add extra punch and excitement to a mix, as well as add prominence to certain sounds by dynamically bringing them to the fore.

Compression is a great tool for enabling you to make the most of the recording headroom available to you, and it can also create the impression of a mix being louder than it really is. Heavy-metal and rock records are pretty much always compressed heavily in the mixing and mastering stages to give the impression of 'everything being louder than everything else'. Be aware, however, that once you've recorded an instrument compressed, it can't be uncompressed, so be careful not to get too extreme with it during the recording process. If you want more compression, you can always add it when mixing and fine-tune the sound further.

These days, more and more studios are going digital, and most home studios are too, but musicians are still seeking the warmth and fatness that came with old analogue tape and vintage equipment that is partly gained from tape saturation and glowing valves. Many recording programs have simulated plug-ins that recreate this, but for more of the real flavour, try running your signal through a preamp or compressor containing valves, such as the TLA Fatman, TLA 5051 or TLA EQ1.

EQ In Studio Recording And Mixing

Thanks to good source sounds and quality mics, instruments and vocals are mostly recorded flat (ie without added EQ), with EQ being applied later to compensate for discrepancies in setups and substandard equipment during the recording process, or to enhance certain lost frequencies. However, EQ should always be used sparingly in order to maintain a natural sound. In the recording and mixing stages, EQ can be used to separate instruments, bringing more clarity to a crowded mix.

Ideally, it's best to start off by using cuts in EQ rather than boosts, as this makes the sound more natural. For instance, when listening to the instrument and trying to make it more prominent, try reducing the top or bottom end to stop the respective frequencies from clashing with the other instruments that reside in the same tonal area. Sometimes you have to add EQ when the sound is missing something that makes it lose itself in the mix.

Occasionally, removing frequencies can make an instrument sound radically different in tone and wrong on its own, but when this instrument is added to the mix, it fits in perfectly because the other instruments around it are occupying the frequencies that it is missing, thus creating an overall tonal balance that sounds correct. An example of this is removing bottom end and lower mids from an acoustic guitar to remove muddiness in a track while the guitar maintains its character. Adding more mid-range frequencies to a rock-guitar sound and reducing its top end also makes it fatter and enables it to sit in the track without blending into the cymbals too much.

Equalising Guitars

Here's a rough guide to using EQ when you're dealing with guitars, but bear in mind that these are only guidelines. You should always trust your ears as well!

- **30Hz–75Hz** – This area isn't used much at all – in fact, normal guitar doesn't often go this low. You can, therefore, often get rid of this.

- **75Hz–150Hz** – This area is usually filtered out to some degree using a low-pass filter. You might not want to get rid of it all, but losing some of it helps – particularly with getting rid of earth hum that may be present in the signal (often in the 100–150Hz area).

- **75Hz–200Hz** – Most rhythm guitar, particularly pop and rock chord playing on the top four strings, doesn't need these frequencies. However, if you're using the low strings, you may like to leave some in or roll some out with a low-frequency filter.

- **200Hz–300Hz** – Often, there isn't much to do here. However, if you're using a small amp this band of frequencies can be made to sound a little fatter by boosting gently at around 150Hz.

- **300Hz–600Hz** – This is the lower-mid area. If you don't want the rhythm guitar to clash with the keyboards, you're best off removing some EQ here. Conversely, this band can be boosted to thicken up some sounds.

- **600Hz–800Hz** – This is the area that, if used excessively, can make guitars sound 'boxy'. Usually there's not a whole lot to do in this area – unless this type of characteristic is desired, of course. Glassy, clean guitar sounds often have some of this removed, too.

- **800Hz–1kHz** – This is the area where honk lives! If you want this type of mid range, dial it in. If not, leave it flat or roll off just a touch. (For glassy, clean sounds you may want to remove a little of this, too.)

- **1kHz–2kHz** – Here we arrive at the centre of the mid range. Often there's nothing to be done here, but it's still a good idea to use your ears to decide. Humbuckers sometimes need to be cut a little here. Incidentally, this area is where all the 'telephone' frequencies are!

- **2kHz–3.5kHz** – This is the area to cut or boost in order to make guitars stand out or sit back in a mix. Also, it's a good place to emphasise muted guitars. Be careful in this area, though, as these frequencies can be painful if too prominent when played loud.

- **3.5kHz–5kHz** – This is the area where sheen lives. Good guitar sounds often have this present anyway, but if you find it needs boosting, you can do so without much problem as it won't clash with vocals or most other instruments.

- **5kHz–8kHz** – This is another place where sheen resides and is a great area to add to dark humbucking-type guitar sounds, particularly if the guitars are strung with heavy-gauge strings or are detuned.

- **8kHz–12kHz** – Now we're up in the 'air' part of the sound. Be a little careful with this area as it can often emphasise pickup noise. However, on a well-recorded, relatively noise-free sound, it can be nice to mix in some extra.

- **12kHz-plus** – Bats and young children can hear this, but for practical guitar purposes it's heading out of any useful range. Cymbals and other high-frequency sounds have some of their sonic information residing up here as well.

Recording With Effects

There are two ways of recording guitars with effects. The first way is to record them dry, without any effects, and then add these later in the mix. For example, a delay, reverb, chorus and so on can be added at the mixing stage to help blend the guitars together and get them to sit right in the mix, to a degree that suits the other elements. This approach has the benefit of flexibility; if you add too much of these effects in the recording process, you're stuck with them and they may prove problematic in the mix. On the other hand, if you have a part that depends on the integral sound of pedals or effects, this will be hard to recreate later with studio gear and techniques, so it's best to commit them to tape or hard disk when actually recording them. But a good point to remember is that a mad live effect may be a bit too over the top and become distracting on a record, so it's up to you to use your judgement and discretion to tone them down accordingly, if necessary.

You can also add effects such as delay and reverb to the aux send of the desk and help the mood of your playing without actually recording them. Sometimes, reverbs such as amp-spring and variable-tape delays are better captured at the time, as they maybe difficult to recreate afterwards. Just be aware that, once you've recorded effects on guitar, you can't change them afterwards, so think about what you want and how you're going to mix it later.

Recording Vocals

As mentioned earlier, when setting up for a vocalist it's important to create a good environment in order to capture a good vibe. This is the icing on the cake after all your hard work tracking! Spend a little time getting a good headphone mix at the right volume and with all the right elements for the singers to pitch to. A mix that's too loud can make the vocalist pitch flat, while a mix that's too quiet can make them pitch sharp, so be warned!

Vocals are best recorded dry in a dead space that has no reflection or natural reverb, which can – and indeed should – be added to the headphone mix if it makes the vocalist more comfortable and not committed to tape or hard disk. Acoustically controlled booths usually create a dead space in professional studios, but you can create your own dead space at home easily enough with duvets hung around and behind the mic. Condenser and cardioid microphones will pick up more sound from the area from behind the vocalist.

Sometimes you can experience popping from certain words beginning with or containing P and B sounds, and this can be controlled by the use of something called a *pop shield*. These can be bought from a store or made from a pair of tights wrapped around a hoop of coat-hanger wire. The shield is positioned about 2–4 inches from the mic, and the vocalist should be around 4–6 inches from the pop shield.

Another occupational hazard is sibilance (the hissing sound created by pronunciation of words beginning with or containing the letter S), which can often be filtered out later in the mixing stage by a unit called a *de-esser*.

Reverb In Mixing

Reverb is explained in Chapter 1, but as well as being important in terms of being applied to guitars, it is also a vital mix tool. Reverb helps to create the overall three-dimensional sound picture in the mixing stage, giving a front-to-back perspective within the sounds of the track. We all know by now that the more reverb we add, the further away the instrument sounds. This means that reverb can help to place instruments spatially in places during a track so that they come back and create a live-sounding and more natural recording.

The applications of reverb on professional recordings has varied over the years, with the '80s being the worst offender for over-use. These days, mixes tend to be a lot drier, giving a more intimate, closer feel. Beginners tend to pile on far too much reverb, which can make the mix sound messy and cloudy by taking up all the space in the track, swamping it and robbing it of most of the definition, making it 'swimmy' or 'too wet'.

It's usually best to start with the drums and work up from there. You'll then be able to tell as you go along where and when you need to add it. It's also a good idea to study other current, well-recorded CDs of similar styles and compare them to your mix.

Panning And Instrument Placement

It's common practise to pan (ie place to either side in a stereo image) guitars and other instruments within a stereo mix in order to create space and clarity so that instruments can be heard separately and, therefore, more prominently. Separate guitar rhythm tracks can be panned left and right to varying degrees to create width, clarity and excitement while hooks and backing vocals can be set to separate sides in order to give more dimension and become more attention-grabbing. Low-frequency sounds such as kick drum and bass guitar are mostly placed in the centre with the lead vocal (or main melody, if it's an instrumental piece), so that their energy driving the track is divided equally and remains constant. Other instruments can then be placed around them, giving the mix dimension and spread.

Be sure to balance the sides of the stereo image equally – listen carefully and check the output meter levels. Again, headphones are good for fine detail and tweaks when it comes to this point.

Finally, when you think you have a good spread, try listening to it in mono to see how it would sound if it was played on a portable radio or an older TV.

Using Automation Within A Mix

By the time you've got this far in a recording and mix, the use of automation is fairly obvious and you probably have a good idea about which parts of the song you want to raise or lower for certain instruments. The 'Flying Fader' system on desks – or digital automation systems on computer setups – will enable you to record individual volume changes within the track.

Generally, drums and bass, if well balanced, stay at the same level throughout the song, retaining the natural dynamics of the performance. Other instruments can be boosted or cut to create dynamics and moods. Vocals can often need 'riding' in order to be made more or less prominent in certain sections, such as at the beginnings of verses, choruses and middle-eights.

If you have a track that's plagued with breathing, hiss or other noise, you can mute it out until it needs to come in. Watch out with drum tracks, though, as the mics on separate drum tracks pick up the other drums in the kit and give the overall sound, so sometimes muting a track can cause dropouts in volume and ambience.

Mastering Tips

The concept of mastering was explained in Chapter 12, but here are some tips on using it for yourself after a mix. Bear in mind that, even though you may constantly check the EQ during the mix and compare your track to other CDs, your ears may tire and monitoring systems may differ, so mastering is your last chance to do any final adjustments before the track is pressed.

The best way to use EQ is with your ears, adjusting it until it sounds right. First, listen to the track and decide what's missing. As a rough guide, a gentle boost in the top end between 6kHz and 10kHz can add a nice sparkle, while a cut in the 1kHz–3kHz range can reduce harshness. Muddiness can be reduced with a cut at around 300Hz, and a little bit of bass punch can be added at around 75Hz–80Hz.

Most mastering is done within computer programs these days, but you can also use standalone units such as the TC Electronic Finalizer and the Focusrite MixMaster.

As explained earlier, compression and limiting are usually added at the end of the process in order to obtain maximum volume and to smoothe out the mix dynamically. Multi-band compressors are often used to compress specific frequency bands within the music, enabling you to compress only the top or bottom end, for example. Listen carefully to avoid distortion or a 'sucking' effect where the compressor is working too hard. If you're going to take your track to a professional mastering house, they are probably going to be happier applying the compression there as they will have way more accurate monitors and also more experience to know the correct amount to add.

And Finally...

Always push yourself to achieve the best performance you can. Once your track is recorded and mixed, it's there forever, and it's always good to walk away feeling that you couldn't have done it any better! Spend plenty of time planning your performance and the recording process, as time well spent then will save heartache later on.

16 LEFTFIELD EFFECTS: PHILOSOPHY AND OTHER USES

In this chapter we thought we'd bring some philosophical thoughts and reasoning behind effects pedals and their roles in the world in a more informal, funky way. By now, you've gained the knowledge about how they work and should be putting them to good use. Here, we question and explore other uses, creative secrets and intuitive techniques that you'll never ever find in a manual!

Creating New Sounds

Remember when you were young and everything was new and exciting? It made life a thrilling journey of exploration and expectation. Even now, to experience something for the first time is fascinating and very gratifying. That's why children are happy and amused by the world and its contents. As we get older, we have experienced so much that it's not so often that we come across something new. That's why, when we do, we're blown away by it and experience a child-like feeling of gratification and thrilling fulfilment.

By the same token, creating and discovering new sounds after years of guitar playing keeps you stimulated thrilled and driven like a child. Yes, new stomp boxes are our gateways back to the innocence and excitement of a child. When we discover a new sound or pedal, it makes us feel good and gives us a reason to carry on. Checking out new pedals is essential to retaining youth, excitement and modernity in your music – and it's also good for your soul!

Recording Acoustic Guitar

One really great trick to use for recording acoustic guitar is to put up two mics spaced exactly on either side of the guitarist. This gives a wide ambient stereo signal – kind of like using overheads on drums. After that, put up one fairly close mic which you pan to the centre in order to capture the detail of the nearfield 'close' sound. All three of these sources are commonly condenser mics that go into a valve preamp and then straight into the recording machine. The blend of these three mics usually gives a pretty large, wide and detailed sound that sounds fine dry or with just a touch of reverb or ambience added to the overheads.

The final thing to do – and this is the secret – is to add the DI pickup sound from the guitar and send it directly to the desk/recorder. Then, during the mixing stage, use it as an FX send only to a stereo reverb. This enables you to add a large spatial reverb which you can then blend in with the original three mic sources. Because the other three signals are quite dry, this other, really wet signal adds the reverb in with them in a way that is really quite unique. If you imagine a busy piece of music that has all the definition, stereo width and detail there but yet still has a great reverb going on too, you'll get the picture of what we're talking about. Phil used this technique on Adrian Legg's 2003 *Guitar Bones* CD and also on Eric Roche's *Perculator* and *Spin* CDs, too. Try it – it works great!

One final word of warning, though: you must be careful to avoid phasing problems when using this many mics plus the DI, although careful mic positioning during the setup stage usually gets around this difficulty. If you do have any problems, though, you can always reverse the polarity on one of the two overhead mics.

Using Digital Cameras

Digital cameras can be a lifesaver for us pedal-board freaks and studio owners. Why? Well, because they enable you to take photos very quickly of things like mic positions and so on. So many times in the past we've spent ages getting the perfect mic position and then someone has walked past and accidentally kicked the stand and moved the mic, or the nuts in the mic stand have loosened and the mic has dropped down. If any of this happens now, we just whip out the camera and have a look at the original mic positions. We can then put them back exactly where they were supposed to be. Great!

Another use for digital cameras is taking pictures of all your pedals after you've laid them out ready to go onto a pedal board. As you try out different orders and placements, you can take pictures of each. You can then easily go back and look at them at your leisure and decide which layout will potentially work best for you. Nothing is worse than the alternative of trying out loads of different arrangements and then forgetting the great layout you had earlier on.

Creating Effects From The Guitar

There are lots of great sound effects that you can achieve just by playing the guitar in an unconventional way. Here are a few of our favourite ideas to get you started:

- Hold a cordless drill, cordless shaver, vibrator(!) – anything with a non-mains-powered motor in it – away from the guitar, turn it on and bring it into close proximity with the strings, then turn it off and on again repeatedly while simultaneously moving it away from the guitar. Instant sonic mayhem and gratification!

- Cross any pair of strings over each other at any fret and hold them down at the exact point where they meet for instant church-bell-type noises. (This one sounds great with lots of reverb added to it as well.)

- Try using different materials for picks, such as bone or metal, or try rubbing different materials on the strings, like tin foil or something similar. Scrape-type effects always sound great when you use metal objects or picks.

- Try picking with the pick sideways to the string(s). This is particularly good for achieving a budget-Mellotron effect, especially if you apply it to double stops and pick close to the bridge. Wicked!

Strange Sounds Within Recordings

Here's a seemingly small topic that can make a huge difference to a recording, or even to your own identity as a guitarist. We're talking about those strange alien-type noises that pop up in tracks, adding an extra dimension and a bit of weirdness to embellish the overall song. People have been doing it for years, from Zappa to Rage Against The Machine. It may only be one second's worth, or it could be a background subliminal thing throughout a whole track, but it can be a totally memorable feature.

We've been known to let the line noise of pedals drone through a whole track in order to add atmosphere, or we've just used a short burst of totally unreasonable, piercing, bizarre noises to grab the listeners' attention and throw the track leftfield for a tiny moment. You can get these sounds from one pedal if it's weird enough, but more often than not it's usually a combination of ingredients. Plug in anything that appears funky and then

haphazardly turn up all the parameters on each pedal until a desired effect is achieved. From generating the sonic cataclasm of World War III to a seance with the Smurfs, there's nothing technical about it; it's all about your ears and your imagination.

If you find yourself experiencing too much feedback or uncontrollable noise before the sound in question appears on the track, just drop it in on the track by punching in and out of recording while it's wailing. Alternatively, use a Mute switch or hard noise gate and put it on as an overdub.

This can be an attention-grabbing moment for guitarists to stamp their authority on a tune and pretend that they're really cool! Sometimes it's wacky and wild, and sometimes it can reinforce the seriousness of a tortured lyric (oh, the pain us poor musicians suffer!). Most of all, though, it's real fun and a great buzz when you create a sound from the guitar that you've never heard before.

Always strive to find exciting and fresh sounds to enthral and emancipate. When fantastic clean sounds are sought and discovered, a wave of euphoria washes over everyone as if they've walked through the gates of heaven. But when it comes to fuzzy attacks, the cruellest, nastiest ugliness is the key to setting the blood rushing to the brain and the primeval fires burning inside us. Just watching everyone come alive in the room when one of these deformed, guiltless monsters rears its ugly head via a victimised amplifier is a wondrous experience; almost like an addiction, it's a pleasure one seeks after relentlessly. We recommend one of these moments every few hours to avoid musical cold turkey in the studio!

Using Effects To Emulate Other Instruments

How about a little pedal trickery to help along the recording process and make life more colourful? When we come to recording, we all try to make something interesting and add something fresh to the approach of the guitar, but sometimes it seems as if everything has been done before and we're just rearranging it with different dynamics.

A great way of being inventive and expanding your guitar knowledge and skills is to try to emulate other instrument sounds electronically with weird pedal combinations. They won't sound exactly the same as the original instruments, but you don't have to be an advanced player to get them – which is dead cool, because then it becomes your own sound invention. (This is also great for single guitarists in a band or demoing at home, because you can play the other parts for the overdubs without having to call someone else in, thus increasing your overall musical spectrum.) People are always saying to us, 'Can you make that sound like a organ?' etc, and we pull out a few old strangers from the pedal arsenal and start to experiment until we find something that gets us juicy.

Also, emulating another instruments can make you play in another way that can be really cool and excitingly innovative. For instance, here's a few sounds we got in the studio from just messing around with bands. Any pedals you have will do; just have fun and keep an open mind.

Recipe-Book Examples

- **Ship's Foghorn** – Whammy (down two octaves), Snarling Dogs Fuzz, DOD Milk Box, DD3 BOSS Delay, Dunlop Rotovibe (on tremolo setting).

- **Synth Bass** – Electro-Harmonix Octave Multiplexer, Colorsound Power Boost (and the tone down on the guitar neck pickup).

- **Cello** – Ebow, Fender Twin Reverb, Colorsound Power Boost.

- **Funky Rhodes Piano** – Rotovibe on phaser setting, Pearl Octaver, spring reverb.

- **Retro Organ** – Wah pedal, BOSS Super Phaser, Danecho, Rotovibe.

- **Indian Wail** – Ebow, Wah pedal, Overdrive, Volume pedal swells, reverb, delay.

- **Strings** – Huge reverb with hardly any direct signal, playing chords as swells with a volume pedal.

Pedal Knowledge

We're all born with talent, but musical genius is something we can acquire through knowledge and experience. As they say, 'Who controls the past controls the present, and who controls the present controls the future,' so it's great to have knowledge of both vintage and strange FX for the attack on the world today. But for that surprise attack of the future, you need to be searching constantly and checking out what's new today. If you have enough time to leave no stone unturned, you can be in a very advantageous position in the insanely competitive world we live in. That's why we're always checking out and collecting new pedals. They may not be used today, but they become part of the troops for the surprise night-offensive that could happen at any time. It's like having a secret guerrilla army ready for the musical mutiny, to topple the evil dinosaurs when music becomes stale. Basically, we would say you've got to stay on top to stay at the top.

Other Uses For Acoustic Guitar

We thought we'd share here a little recording trick that can add monstrous fatness to a recording, or alienistic weirdness to get people guessing. You may think we've gone a bit soft mentioning acoustic guitars, but here's a wonderful way to use the old plank for double-tracking rock guitars in the studio. It can add a new dimension in tone and body to rhythm tracks, plus spleen-shaking, original-sounding solos and riffs.

Basically, you need an acoustic guitar with a built-in electric pickup – bridge or soundhole position will do. Plug it into a high-gain channel in your amp and crank that mutha up! Valve heads are the best, but fuzz is fuzz – if you've got the right ear to tweak the EQ, anything can be used. We use Marshall, Orange, Carvin, Laney and Cornford, which all have villainous sounds when cranked up. Stay as far away from the speakers as possible – the feedback can be criminal – and record with the amp in another room via a long guitar lead!

What you do next is double your original electric-guitar rhythm track. The result is a rich, full tone that you couldn't capture with electrics alone – guaranteed crambunctuous elation when the desired effect is nailed.

Next up is adding spice to riffs or solos. How about adding a few FX boxes to the equation? For instance, using Danelectro fuzz boxes or the Snarling Dogs distortions (Fabtone and Tweed E Dog respectively) on a lightly gained valve amp can produce an incredible woody gnarliness with wonderful overtones and harmonics, not to mention feedback from the Lord himself. Doubling a one-string, low riff will give you a sound that will create magnanimous tone envy, and doubling solos has a splendiferous magical reward. And then there are all those other boxes just waiting to corrupt your defenceless, sheltered, virgin acoustic with their sinful pleasures of the wood. The experimentation is endless and gratuitously rewarding.

Capturing Inspiration

Inventing a new killer riff is like Christmas mixed with your birthday and a heroic end to a hot date – all at the same time! But it's easy to forget them at almost the same time as you create them – or wake up the next day and find that the dog has eaten your memory! We're sure you all know exactly what we're talking about!

The secret is to have a bunch of pedals plugged into a cool-sounding amp and jam away, getting ideas, with a multitracker and amp simulator plugged into one track ready to record. When you get a woody groove on and you're lovin' it, just whip out the cable, plug into the multitracker and record the section for a few bars. Always leave the track at the end so that you don't have to waste time cueing it up and losing the ideas that are flowing. Then, move on to new ideas while the force is still flowing.

At a later date, listen back to all the grooves when you're songwriting and relearn them or sample them and drop them straight into a demo for ultimate ease and speed. Sometimes you can cut them in different places and create a whole new feel that is contemporary and unique. It's a really innovative and inspirational way to work.

Creative Sampling

Here's another secret when it comes to recording, songwriting or demo enhancement. Sometimes you need that special touch and extraterrestrial sparkle, like a tasty spice in the cooking pot that's unique and original to you on your track, or maybe an inspiring little ditty to get the creative juices flowing. And, of course, the solution involves our much-loved friends, the stomp army! We set up a load of weird and wonderful amigos all in a line and plug them via an amp simulator into a recording facility. Then, we just zone out and take a trip through insanity to stupidity, making the most crazy and original sounds possible, from feedback to noise and bizarre notes. Even the line noise of certain combinations of boxes can be a wondrous and religious experience.

On other occasions, we sit down with a sampler and cut up all the pieces, create a sample library and store them all on disk. Then it's so simple: every time we have a tune that needs 'a little something for the weekend, Sir', we scan through our libraries until we find a cool sound for the piece and drop it in, sometimes reversed or pitched up or down. This saves loads of time, and it means that quality FX are inserted instead of a five-minute fumbling excuse that lacks resources and imagination. Obviously we don't do this all the time, as it would take the spark out of the recording process, but it's sometimes a great day-saver!

Recording Ultra-Fuzzy Sounds

Lets talk about dirty, filthy, ugly distortion. Not just that of the fuzz-pedal variety, but also that of the total chaos and vileness you can get through studio-recorded trickery. Sometimes you hear a sound so hot and gnarly, it seems as if it has another dimension to it other than just that of an amp and pedal.

A number of factors can be involved and employed in achieving divine badness to the power of X. This can make going up to 11 a weedy wannabe, and all your enemies will crumble into decrepitude trying to compete with your sublime tone mutilation.

A few ingredients are needed for this lethal cocktail. Firstly, you need to lay the foundations by achieving the desired monster tone from your guitar into the amp, and

wind up to about 7 or 8 for that harmonic drive overtone obtained by pushing the output valves. (But don't go to 10 as it may get a bit too 'woolly' and reduce clarity from the end result.) Now add a fuzz or overdrive box with a compressor pedal, pushing the drive up to full to get unreasonable and abusive results.

You may think you're cooking now, but the icing on the cake and that extra dimension comes from the recording process. Mic up the amp well and make sure that the flat (EQ-free) sound of the guitar through the desk is the same as your amp in the live room. Now turn up the input on the desk way into the red – or the needle on the dial way over the limit – so that the recorded signal is distorted (on a valve desk) or clipping on a digital unit. The signal at this stage is overloading and obviously very hot – far too dangerous for BBC-type recording engineers! – but the result, depending on how far you want to push it, is a sonic Stanley knife face-slashing of grievous aural harm. Oh, you may want to use a noise gate if you want sharp vicious stabs (or to control the howl) before or after the miking process.

Digital and valve desks will respond differently, and it's up to you to determine at which point it sounds good or bad as you push the recording input. Give it a try – I guarantee you'll be praising the dark lords if you get it right!

Pedals And Vocal Recordings

In the quest to exploit every possible angle of usage from the wonderful world of stompage, we were wondering if it had crossed your mind to exercise your vocal cords through your boxes on a recording after you've abused and pillaged them on the backing tracks with your fearful axe?

In good studios we have dedicated rack FX for mixing that are technically perfect and clinically designed to do the right thing, but sometimes you want to do the *wrong* thing and obtain a unique vocal sound that can really make the track, capture the moment and stretch the imagination of the listener. It's very common to distort the vocal sound, and we hear this a lot these days – anything from a desk-channel overload to a ten-quid fuzz pedal. But the real fun starts when you get a bit more creative and a few more original combinations are employed.

Don't be scared to plug in anything and give it a go. From four-track machines to huge production studios, it doesn't matter how you achieve the end result as long as it sounds good. Not long ago we put a voice through a Snarling Dogs Wah and a Danecho and, through tweaking them, discovered a fantastic texture for a dub-reggae track. A Small Stone phaser can give a watery feel to a lead vocal, and a BOSS Super Phaser speeded up with a BOSS DD3 delay can give haunting backing melodies. Meanwhile, subtle flangers can give a cold, hollow, divorced ambience, and a cranked Electric Mistress could provoke a response from an alien civilisation.

If you're feeling demonic, you could try adding a pitch shifter or a BOSS Octave with a DOD overdrive, but for original nuttiness, ring modulation (Lovetone Ring Stinger or DOD Gonkulator) with a phaser or flanger could create the new Frankenstein's monster. It's all fun and highly creative, producing uniqueness in abundance. The possibilities are endless and emancipating!

Reasons To Carry On

It's very rare that we have days when we say, 'Fuck it. What's the point of endless hours of questioning and searching for the ultimate sound?', but if we ever do – which I suppose we all do at some point in our lives – we only have to hear one great record or see a fantastic live band and we're full of inspiration and fuelled up again instantly. Because we both started playing the guitar when we were very young years ago, it's one of the only things we do that instantly takes us back and makes us feel like that child again. It's kind of like eating sweets that you ate when you were a kid – the flavour comes flooding back and you feel all little again! I'm sure John Lee Hooker felt that way, even though he was still gigging at the age of 83! So, instead of calling the classifieds and shifting mountains of dusty disturbers of the peace, we get down to a few gigs or slap on our Walkmans and wander around the park with a classic CD to give us more fire and movement than Mount Etna on a bad day.

17 EFFECTS AND GUITAR-HERO TRACKS

Here's a whole bunch of classic tracks that recognisably feature the effects that we talk about in this book. Of course, there are millions of songs out there awash with crazy stuff and subtle overtones, but these are some of the artists that we have encountered who inspire us, listed in alphabetical order by name.

Ace

Ace, from Skunk Anansie and AceSounds (and, of course, co-author of this book), uses many special effects, from well-known classics to weird and unique combinations. Tracks to check out include the tremolo on 'And This Is Nothing' and 'Tracy's Floor', and octave with pitch shifter on 'Charlie Big Potato' from the Skunk Anansie *Post-Orgasmic Chill* album. Have a listen to the AceSounds album *Still Hungry* for an example of a square-wave-tremolo/pan-effect intro and a whammy solo on the track 'There's No Pleasing Some People', a backwards warp solo on 'This Is The Last Time', plus the hard-gating-and-envelope-filter intro on 'Your Face Hurts'.

Wes Borland

Limp Bizkit's Wes Borland uses many effects on the *Chocolate Starfish And The Hot Dog Flavored Water* LP including envelope filter and preamps on 'Hot Dog'.

Vigilante Carlstroem

The Hives' Vigilante Carlstroem uses a heavy fuzz sound on the riff to 'Hate To Say I Told You' from the *Your New Favourite Band* LP.

Richard Carpenter

Richard Carpenter, from – you guessed it – the Carpenters, uses a vintage fuzz for the solo on 'Goodbye To Love'.

Kurt Cobain

Kurt Cobain, of Nirvana fame, used a Univibe for the rhythm verses and solo on 'Smells Like Teen Spirit', from the *Nevermind* album.

Phil Collen/Steve Clarke

Phil Collen and Steve Clarke (RIP), from Def Leppard, use detune and chorus a lot on their many LPs. One good example is 'Love Bites', from the *Hysteria* album.

Eddie Clarke/Phil Campbell

'Fast' Eddie Clarke and Phil Campbell from Motörhead have used wah-pedal effects for many solos throughout the years. A good example is the wah solo on 'The Ace Of Spades', from the LP of the same title.

Billy Corgan

Billy Corgan, of Smashing Pumpkins, used the Electro-Harmonix Micro Synthesizer to great effect on many songs. A couple of good examples are 'Quiet' and 'Hummer' from *Siamese Dream*.

Billy Duffy

Billy Duffy, of The Cult, obtained post-gothic rock tones using flangers. Check out 'She Sells Sanctuary' and others from the *Love* LP.

The Edge

U2's The Edge has always experimented with effects, so it's worth checking out everything he's done. For good use of the whammy, check out the intro to 'Even Better Than The Real Thing' from *Achtung Baby*. Also the use of a TC Electronic 2290 on 'Where The Streets Have No Name'.

Peter Frampton

Peter Frampton demonstrates early talkbox techniques on his big '70s hit 'Baby I Love Your Way'.

Dave Gilmour

Dave Gilmour is the guitar and effects master in Pink Floyd and has produced many classic sounds over the years. 'Comfortably Numb' from *The Wall* contains his trademark solo sound, utilising both delay and chorus.

Peter Green

Peter Green uses a huge reverb for his melody lines and solo on the classic Fleetwood Mac track 'Albatross', included on their *Greatest Hits* LP.

Eddie Van Halen

Eddie Van Halen used flangers and choruses on many Van Halen tracks over the years. Check out the use of flanger in varying degrees on 'Unchained' (from the album *Women And Children First*) and 'Atomic Punk' from *Van Halen II*. He also demonstrates a fantastic use of a modified Echoplex delay and volume control on the track 'Cathedral', from *Diver Down*.

Peter Hayes

Peter Hayes, from Black Rebel Motor Cycle Club, uses many vintage effects on their self-titled debut LP. For example, check out the ring modulator on the intro to 'Whatever Happened To My Rock And Roll?'.

Jimi Hendrix

Jimi Hendrix was the original effects guru, and there are many tracks to check out to hear his creative use of all the early '60s and '70s vintage effects. Fuzz and wah are featured on many tracks, such as 'Voodoo Chile', and all of his LPs. A backwards guitar solo features on 'Castles Made Of Sand', from *Axis: Bold As Love*.

The Isley Brothers

The Isley Brothers demonstrate a fantastic fuzz-pedal intro solo on the classic 'Summer Breeze'.

John 5

John 5, from Marilyn Manson's band, demonstrates heavy compressor and preamp use on many songs, including 'The Fight Song' on the *Holy Wood* LP.

Richard Kruspe/Paul Landers

Richard Kruspe and Paul Landers, of Rammstein, use SansAmp preamps to obtain really heavily distorted riffs on all of their LPs. For example, check out the rhythm sounds on 'Du Hast', from *Sehnsucht*.

Alex Lifeson

Rush's Alex Lifeson always used a volume pedal to great effect. A great example is '2112' from the Rush *2112* LP.

Marcos

Marcos, from POD, demonstrates the power of hard noise gating on many tracks on the band's *Satellite* LP. For an example, listen to the rhythm guitars on 'Set It Off' and 'Boom'.

Martha And The Muffins

Martha and the Muffins created a legendary intro to their hit single 'Echo Beach' using an '80s chorus effect.

Hank Marvin

Hank Marvin got his legendary trademark sound from a Meazzi slapback echo dating from 1958.

Brian May

Queen six-stringer Brian May pioneered many trademark effects sounds over the years. His use of Echoplex tape delays on 'Brighton Rock', from Queen's *Sheer Heart Attack* album, is amazing – as, of course, is the unforgettable guitar synth solo on 'I Want To Break Free' from *The Works*.

Tom Morello

Tom Morello, of Rage Against The Machine, redefined creative effect use and techniques in the early '90s. All of the RATM LPs are an FX-fest. Check out the wah on the intro riff of 'Bulls On Parade', from *Evil Empire*, and the all-time classic whammy solo on 'Killing In The Name Of' from *Rage Against The Machine*.

Munky, Head

Korn's Munky and Head are incredible users of multi-FX and create many unique sounds on all of their records, which are well worth checking out. An example of a great envelope-filter intro can be heard on 'Justin', from *Follow The Leader*.

Jimmy Page

Jimmy Page, of Led Zeppelin, demonstrates a great wah-solo hook melody in 'No Quarter', from *Houses Of The Holy*. He also used many effects, including a rotary speaker, on 'Down By The Seaside' and a phaser on 'Ten Years Gone' (from *Physical Graffiti*). Led Zeppelin featured many innovative effects of their era.

Pepper Keenan

Pepper Keenan, of Corrosion Of Conformity, shows the use of Fat Stoner-style fuzz on the opening riff and rhythm guitars of 'Albatross', from *Deliverance*.

Jeff Rose

Jeff Rose, of Skindred, uses the DigiTech whammy to classic octave-shifting use on the opening riff to 'Pressure', from the *Babylon* LP.

Ritchie Sambora

Ritchie Sambora, of Bon Jovi fame, brings the '70s talkbox back to life on the hook-line melody of their hit 'Living On A Prayer'.

Brian Setzer

Brian Setzer, of The Stray Cats, used a vintage slapback delay setting on a Roland Space Echo.

Slash

Slash, of Guns N' Roses and Snakepit, is renowned for his wah solo sound as featured on the all-time classic 'Sweet Child Of Mine', from *Appetite For Destruction*.

John Spencer

John Spencer, from Blues Explosion, uses many combinations of vintage pedals to create bizarre and unorthodox sounds, and to compensate for the lack of a bass player In the band. LPs to check out are *Extra Width*, *Acme*, *Now I Got Trouble* and *Orange*.

Andy Summers

Andy Summers, of The Police, demonstrates great use of chorus and delay on 'Walking On The Moon', and flanger on the intro to 'Bring On The Night', from *Regatta de Blanc*.

Steve Vai

Steve Vai demonstrates many uses of pitch-shifting solos on his *Passion And Warfare* LP.

Stevie Ray Vaughan

Stevie Ray Vaughan uses a rotary speaker for the opening of 'Cold Shot'.

Joe Walsh

Joe Walsh, of The Eagles' six-stringers, shows us a fantastic example of a talkbox solo on his '70s solo hit 'Rocky Mountain Way'.

Angus Young

Angus Young, the extremely active axeman with rockers AC/DC, never uses any effects pedals in his setup and plainly illustrates the use of a good Marshall amplifier preamp on all of their albums. For a classic AC/DC tone, we recommend checking out the *Highway To Hell* and live *If You Want Blood* CDs.

18 MUSIC NOTATION

CD Track 21a (chapter 6)

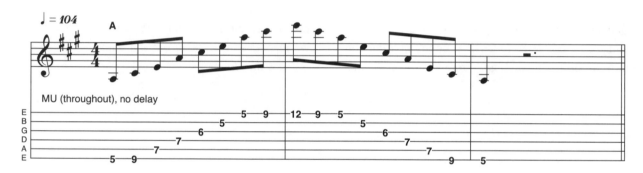

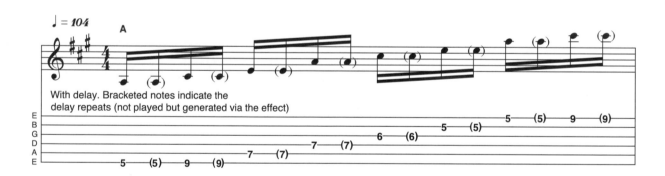

CD Track 21b (Chapter 6)

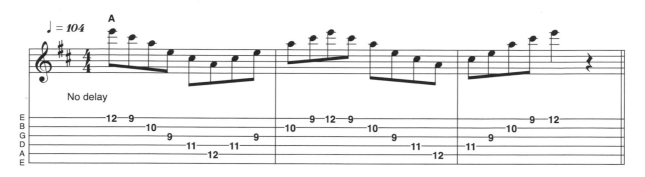

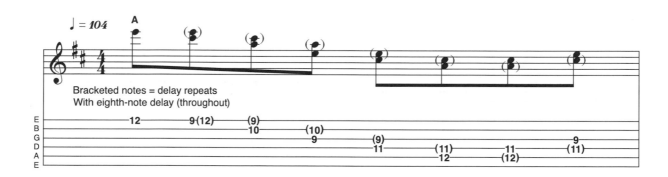

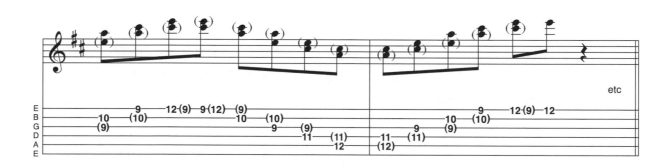

CD Track 21c (Chapter 6)

Scale in 3rds (with delay). Bracketed notes = delay repeats.

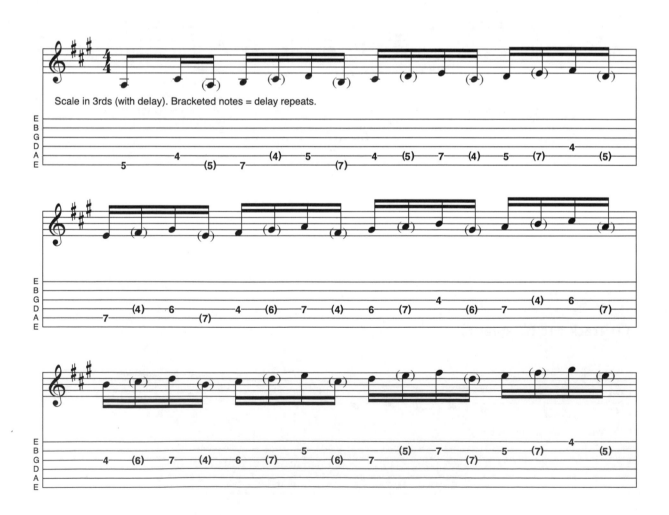

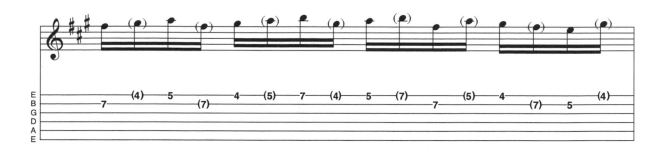

Delay Examples Footnote

To work out delay times for yourself, try the following calculations:

♩. = Divide 45000 by the tempo of the music

♩ = Divide 45000 by the tempo of the music

♪ = Divide 45000 by the tempo of the music

Chapter 16: Track 54e, '3b Harmonics'

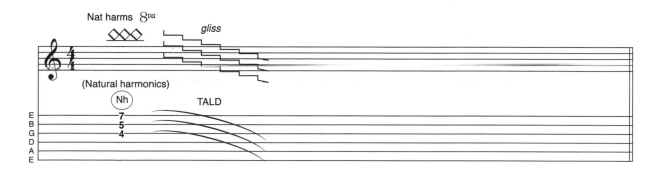

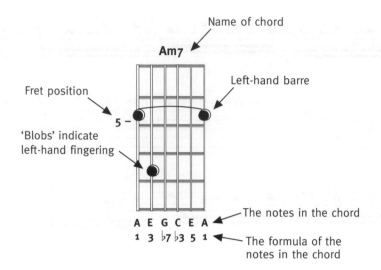

Name of chord

Am7

Left-hand barre

Fret position

5 –

'Blobs' indicate left-hand fingering

The notes in the chord

A E G C E A

1 3 ♭7 ♭3 5 1

The formula of the notes in the chord

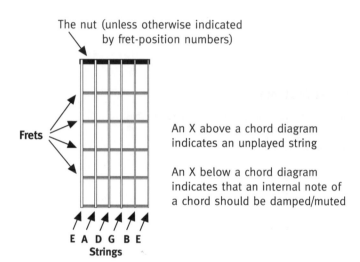

The nut (unless otherwise indicated by fret-position numbers)

Frets

E A D G B E
Strings

An X above a chord diagram indicates an unplayed string

An X below a chord diagram indicates that an internal note of a chord should be damped/muted

Rock Chord Forms – For Distorted Sounds

The following chord forms are great for use with any distorted effects.
They do, of course, sound fine with a clean tone as well.

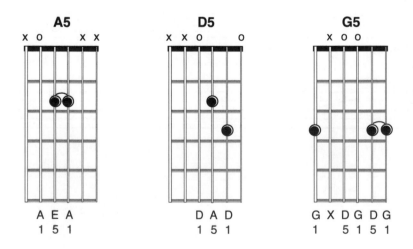

A5

X O   X X

A E A
1 5 1

D5

X X O   O

D A D
1 5 1

G5

X O O

G X D G D G
1   5 1 5 1

E5

E	B	E	X	B	E
1	5	1		5	1

F5
(moveable)

F	C	F
1	5	1

B5
(moveable)

B	F♯	B
1	5	1

Csus2

C	X	G	D
1		5	2/9

Csus2

C	G	C	D	G
1	5	1	2/9	5

A5

A	E	A	E	A
1	5	1	5	1

G/B

B	D	G	D	G
3	5	1	5	1

Gm/B♭

B♭	D	G	D	G
♭3	5	1	5	1

Asus4

A	E	A	D
1	5	1	4

D/A
(A6sus4)

x o   o

A F♯ A D
1 6 1 4(of A)

A7sus4

x o

A E A D G
1 5 1 4 ♭7

D5

x x o

D A D A
1 5 1 5

Bsus4

x   o o

B F♯ B B E
1 5 1 1 4

E5

o   o o

7 –

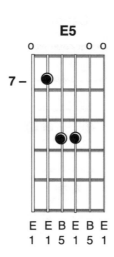

E E B E B E
1 1 5 1 5 1

D5 add6/9

x   o o

D A D B E
1 5 1 6 9

Cmaj7

x   o o

C G B B E
1 5 7 7 3

F♯7/11

x   o o

F♯ X F♯ A♯ B E
1   1 3 11 ♭7

A5

x   x

7 –

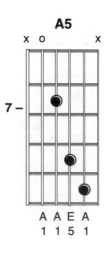

A A E A
1 1 5 1

Fmaj7♭5

F   F A B E
1   1 3 ♭5 7

G5/E

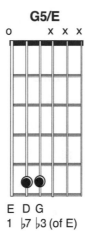

E D G
1 ♭7 ♭3 (of E)

F♯5/E

E C♯ F♯
1 6 9 (of E)

A/C♯

C♯ A
3 1

E5/6

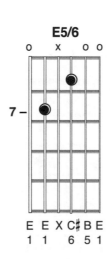

E E X C♯ B E
1 1 6 5 1

E5/♭7

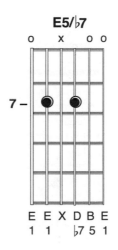

E E X D B E
1 1 ♭7 5 1

E7♯9

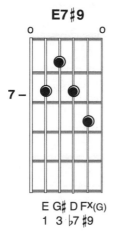

E G♯ D Fˣ(G)
1 3 ♭7 ♯9

A7♯9

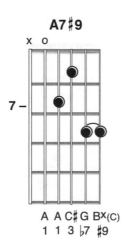

A A C♯ G Bˣ(C)
1 1 3 ♭7 ♯9

E (♭5)

E B♭ E B♭
1 ♭5 1 ♭5

The following chord forms all sound great with clean sounds and with effects such as chorus, flange, delay and reverb. Some of them also are fine with crunch and distorted tones. Experiment!

Em9

```
E  B  E  G  D  F#
1  5  1  b3 b7 9
```

Em9

```
E  B  F# G  D  E
1  5  9  b3 b7 1
```

Amaj add9

```
A  E  B  C# E
1  5  9  3  5
```

Am add9

```
A  E  B  C  E
1  5  9  b3 5
```

Gm6

```
G  X  D  Bb D  E
1     5  b3 5  6
```

Emaj add9

```
E  B  F# G# B  E
1  5  9  3  5  1
```

E/G#

```
G# X  E  B  E
3     1  5  1
```

Em/G

```
G  X  E  B  E
b3    1  5  1
```

F#m7/11

```
F# X  E  A  B  E
1     b7 b3 11 b7
```

Dsus2

x x o   o

D A D E
1 5 1 2/9

Am9

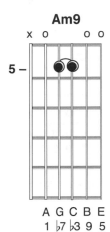

x o   o o

5 –

A G C B E
1 ♭7 ♭3 9 5

Amaj add9

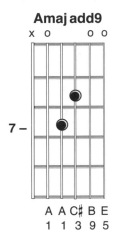

x o   o o

7 –

A A C♯ B E
1 1 3 9 5

Am add9

x o   o o

7 –

A A C B E
1 1 ♭3 9 5

C♯m7

x   o o

C♯ E B B E
1 ♭3 ♭7 ♭7 ♭3

Asus2

x o   o o

A E A B E
1 5 1 2/9 5

Bm7/11

x   o o

7 –

B A D B E
1 ♭7 ♭3 1 11

Cmaj7

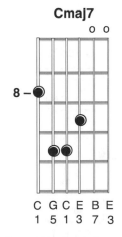

o o

8 –

C G C E B E
1 5 1 3 7 3

Em9

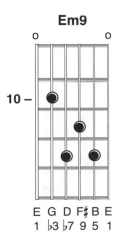

o   o

10 –

E G D F♯ B E
1 ♭3 ♭7 9 5 1

Note: This chord shape also
works great when played at
frets 12, 10, 7, 5, 3, 2 and 1

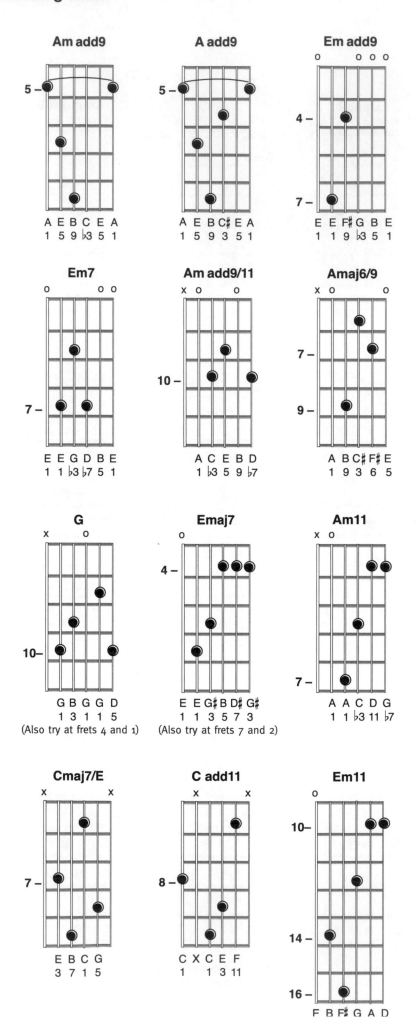

RESOURCES

Here are a few web addresses for effects manufacturers and other selected retailers.

Ace And Phil
www.acesounds.com
www.philhilborne.com

Pedals And Multi-FX
www.dod.com
www.digitech.com
www.danelectro.com
www.jhs.co.uk
www.voodoolab.com
www.prosoundcommunications.com
www.ts808.com
www.line6.com
www.carlmartin.com
www.marshallamps.com
www.ibanez.com
www.roger-mayer.co.uk
www.jimdunlop.com
www.fulltone.com
www.ehx.com
www.visualsound.net
www.frantone.com
www.BOSSfx.com
www.t-rex-eng.com
www.yamaha-music.co.uk
www.zvex.com
www.lehle.com
www.ebs.bass.se/
www.imentryimports.co.uk
www.zoom.co.jp
www.realmccoycustom.com
www.morleypedals.com
www.rolandus.com
www.voxamps.co.uk

www.aphex.com
www.lovetone.com
www.hughes-and-kettner.com

Rack Preamps And Pedals
www.vhtamp.com
www.badcatamps.com
www.koch-amps.com
www.tech21nyc.com

Rack Units, Modelling Units And Pedals
www.korg.co.uk
www.gibsonechoplex.com
www.BBEsound.com
www.behringer.com
www.line6.com/variax
www.roland.co.uk
www.tcelectronic.com
www.rogerlinndesign.com

Pedal Boards
www.pedaltrain.com

Retailers
www.soundsgreatmusic.com
www.pmtonline.co.uk

Amps, Guitars And Miscellaneous
www.cornfordamps.com
www.prsguitars.com
www.fret-king.com
www.celestian.com
www.marshallamps.com
www.picato.co.uk
www.tascam.co.uk
www.bimm.co.uk

ABOUT THE AUTHORS

Ace

Ace is the former guitarist and songwriter with rock band Skunk Anansie. With the release of the LPs *Paranoid And Sunburnt*, *Stoosh* and *Post-Orgasmic Chill*, the band clocked up worldwide sales of over 4 million and sold out venues all over the world. A couple of career highlights include headlining The Glastonbury Festival in 1999, and in 1998 being asked by Nelson Mandela to play his 'Gift To The Nation' 80th birthday show in South Africa.

Now he is a solo artist in his own right with his AceSounds LP *Still Hungry* and establishing himself as an up-and-coming record producer and songwriter. As well as these achievements, Ace has been the main touring DJ and compere for the *Kerrang!* magazine Club tours, Monsters Of Rock tour, Download Festival and Game On.

Ace is also a guest lecturer at the Brighton Institute of Modern Music, the Academy of Contemporary Music and the Brit School, teaching all aspects of guitar techniques, recording and survival in the music business. He also has been writing a column on effects pedals for *Guitarist* magazine for the past few years.

Ace has been inducted into the Marshall players' Roll of Honour and holds the Guinness world record for the most effects pedals ever played simultaneously!

Phil Hilborne

Phil Hilborne has established himself as one of the most respected and versatile guitarists of the past 20 years. His contributions to the guitar world have ranged from fronting his own Phil Hilborne Band to teaching, producing and music editing, working as a session musician, recording artist, composer, journalist, author and much more.

Phil was the first person ever to write a regular rock-guitar instruction article in a UK magazine ('Playing Rock Guitar' – *Guitarist* magazine, 1985–95), during which time he developed a tab standard that is now widely used across the globe. Since 1994 he has been an integral part of the *Guitar Techniques* magazine team, working as music editor and producing/recording over 100 CDs for *GT* alone.

He has performed many live demonstrations and clinics for leading music companies, including Marshall, Gibson, Ampeg, Cornford, Vigier, Paiste, Sonor, Zildjian, PRS, Washburn, Fender, Seymour Duncan, Larrivée, Beyer Dynamic, Kitty Hawk, Crate, Hohner and Ernie Ball.

For the past 14 years, Phil has also been part of Iron Maiden drummer Nicko McBrain's touring clinic band and has done many successful gigs/tours with him, including his Rhythms Of The Beast and Return Of The Beast tours, Frankfurt Music Messe (1993, 1994 and 2003) and the London Music Show at Wembley (1993 and 2003), as well as being a regular performer in the Queen musical *We Will Rock You* in London.

Phil has also held numerous guitar clinics and masterclasses in the UK and Europe, including the prestigious Bath International Guitar Festival (1999–2003). He was also a visiting faculty instructor for MI London and the Guitar Institute in Acton, London, and is currently both visiting instructor to and Curriculum Director (Guitar) of the Brighton Institute of Modern Music.

Phil (left) and Ace (right)